Answers

iology

ection 1 — Cells and Respiration

age 9 — Mildly Marvellous icroscope Questions

uick Fire Questions

Making objects look bigger.
It magnifies the object on the slide.
So you can choose how much you want the image to be magnified / how big you want the image to be.

actice Questions

(a)(i) So she can see the different parts of the cells more clearly.
(ii) It protects the object on the slide.
(b)(i) B
(ii) A
(iii)Place the microscope near a lamp or a window, and angle the mirror so light shines up through the hole in the stage.
(iv)E.g. turn the focusing knob so that the objective lens is moving away from the slide. / Angle the mirror so that it's not reflecting direct sunlight into the microscope.
(c) So that light can shine through it.
You need light to shine up from below onto whatever's on your slide, so you can see it more clearly.

ages 11-12 — Seriously Super Cell Questions

uick Fire Questions

nucleus
Most of the reactions for aerobic respiration.
In the chloroplasts. It is needed for photosynthesis.
A living thing made up of only one cell.

ractice Questions

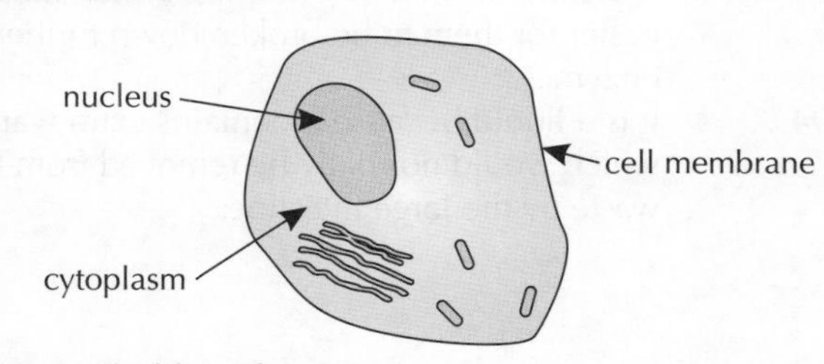

2 (a) a jelly-like substance
(b) e.g. cell wall/vacuole/chloroplast

3

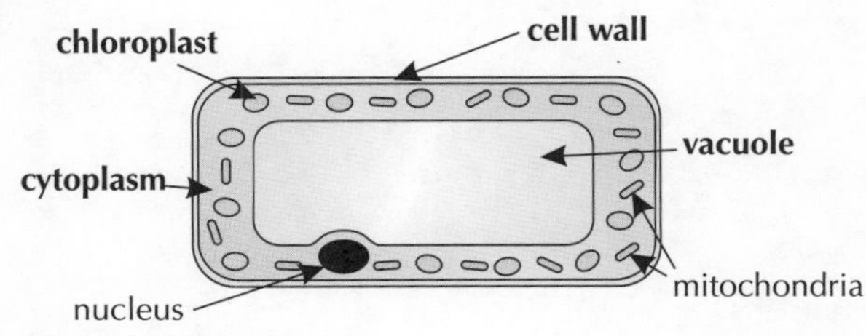

4 (a) the vacuole
(b) cellulose
(c) It supports the cell.

Q5 (a) In the cytop
(b) It holds the
and out of t
(c) E.g. they have a contractile vacuole to squeeze any excess water out of the cell.

Pages 15-16 — Awesomely Original Organisation Questions

Quick Fire Questions

Q1 A group of different tissues that work together.
Q2 A group of organs that work together.
Q3 A substance moves from an area of high concentration to an area of low concentration.

Practice Questions

Q1 similar cells → **tissue** → organ → **organ system** → whole organism
Q2 (a) e.g. leaf
(b) e.g. stomach
There are lots of other answers you could give here.
Q3 In the leaf cells.
Q4 (a) a tissue
(b) inside, membrane, diffusion
Q5 (a) an organ
(b) **1 — a blood cell**, **2 — blood**, **3 — liver**, **4 — digestive system**, 5 — sheep
Q6 The concentration of minerals is higher in the root cell than it is in the soil. If the minerals were moving by diffusion they would pass out of the root cell (the area of high concentration) into the soil (the area of low concentration).

Pages 18-19 — Refreshingly Radical Respiration Questions

Quick Fire Questions

Q1 All of them.
Q2 energy
Q3 glucose → lactic acid (+ energy)

Practice Questions

Q1 It releases the energy organisms need to stay alive.
Q2 mitochondria
Q3 **glucose** + oxygen → **carbon dioxide** + **water** (+ ENERGY)
Q4 more, anaerobically, oxygen
Q5 (a) Glucose, because yeast need glucose to respire.
(b) carbon dioxide
(c) ethanol (alcohol)
(d)(i) The temperature of the water bath.
The independent variable is the thing you change in an experiment.
(ii) Any two from: e.g. the amount of yeast / the type of yeast cells / the amount of glucose / the length of time the bubbles were counted for.
(iii)accurate / repeatable
(e) e.g. beer

Answers

Section 2 — Humans as Organisms

Pages 21-22 — Naturally Nifty Nutrition Questions

Quick Fire Questions

Q1 energy

Q2 E.g. complex carbohydrates release energy slowly, simple carbohydrates release energy quickly. / Complex carbohydrates are found in foods like bread/pasta, simple carbohydrates are found in foods like sweets/fruit.

Q3 For growth and to repair damaged areas / building cells.

Q4 About 75%.

Practice Questions

Q1 (a) E.g. it helps food move through your digestive system. / It stops you getting constipation.
(b) Breakfast cereal, peas, carrots, oats and bananas should be underlined.

Q2 (a) F
(b) T
(c) F
(d) F
(e) T
(f) F
(g) T

Q3 (a) Any two from: e.g. fruits, vegetables, cereals.
(b) E.g. it helps wound healing. / It can help your immune system.
(c) Iron — blood,
Sodium — nerves
Calcium — bones and teeth

Q4 (a) fish
(b) The fish, because saturated fat can be bad for your health / unsaturated fat is better for you than saturated fat.
(c) E.g. she may feel dizzy, tired and have bad headaches.

Page 25 — (More) Naughty But Nice Nutrition Questions

Quick Fire Questions

Q1 Body mass (weight) and level of activity.

Q2 E.g. not getting enough of a certain vitamin or mineral in your diet.

Q3 E.g. scurvy — causes problems with skin, joints and gums. / Iron deficiency anaemia — causes tiredness, lack of energy and shortness of breath.

Practice Questions

Q1 (a) Daily BER (kJ/day) = 5.4 × 24 × 65 = **8424** kJ/day
(b) She has a bigger mass which takes more energy to move and she will have more cells that need more energy.
(c) Energy need for activities = (1700 ÷ 2) + 850
= 1700 kJ
Energy needed in total = 1700 + BER
= 1700 + 8424
= **10 124** kJ/day

Q2 (a) If you eat too much, you might take in more energy than you use up. The body stores the ex energy as fat so you put on weight. This can lea to obesity which can cause health problems suc as high blood pressure and heart disease.
(b) E.g. slow growth (in children), an increased risk infection, irregular periods (in women).

Pages 27-28 — Dazzlingly Dynamic Digestion Questions

Quick Fire Questions

Q1 hydrochloric acid

Q2 e.g. liver and pancreas

Q3 Any two from: mouth, pancreas, small intestine, stomach.

Practice Questions

Q1 1 — mouth — Mixes food with saliva.
2 — oesophagus — Links the mouth to the stomach.
3 — stomach — Contains acid to kill bacteria.
4 — small intestine — Where food is absorbed into the blood.
5 — large intestine — Where water is absorbe
6 — rectum — Temporarily stores and then get rid of undigested food.

Q2 It produces enzymes to break down protein, carbohydrates and fats and releases them into th small intestine.

Q3 (a) Chemical digestion and mechanical digestion.
(b) E.g. muscular tissue moves the stomach wall an churns up food.
(c)(i) Carbohydrates and proteins.
Carbohydrates start to be broken down by an enzyme (amylase) in the mouth and proteins st to be broken down in the stomach by protease enzymes.
(ii) E.g. they speed up the rate of chemical reaction in the body. / They are biological catalysts.
(d)(i) bile
(ii) It breaks fats into tiny droplets which makes it easier for them to be broken down further by enzymes.

Q4 It is a liquid because it contains extra water, which would normally be removed from the waste by the large intestine.

CGP

Key Stage Three
Biology, Physics & Chemistry

Answer Book

For the **Higher Level** Study & Question Books

Contents

Biology

Chemistry

Physics

Published by CGP
From original material by Paddy Gannon
ISBN: 978 1 78294 108 8
www.cgpbooks.co.uk
Printed by Elanders Ltd, Newcastle upon Tyne.
Clipart from Corel®
Based on the classic CGP style created by Richard Parsons

Answers

ages 30-31 — Magnificently Mighty ore on Digestion Questions

uick Fire Questions

1 in the blood

2 villi/villus

actice Questions

1

Feature	Reason it's useful
Provide a large surface area	Increases the number of food molecules that can be absorbed at the same time.
Good blood supply	**Allows food molecules to be absorbed into the blood easily.**
Thin outer layer of cells	**Means the food molecules don't have far to travel to get into the blood.**

2 (a) Yes because bacteria found naturally in the gut can stop harmful bacteria from growing in your intestines so you are less likely to get ill. Bacteria found naturally in the gut can also produce enzymes that can break down structures in plant cells which we couldn't break down otherwise. This means they help with digestion.

(b) E.g. produce useful hormones, make useful vitamins.

3 (a) amylase and maltase

(b) E.g. glucose is a smaller molecule than starch. Glucose is soluble whereas starch is insoluble. *Remember, the reason why molecules need to be broken down in the digestive system is so that they can be absorbed into the blood. Big, insoluble molecules are broken down into smaller, more soluble ones.*

(c) It will be absorbed into the blood and then carried around the body to the cells where it is needed.

ages 33-34 — Simply Splendid keleton and Muscle Questions

uick Fire Questions

1 The skull.

2 true

3 A tough band that attaches a muscle to a bone.

actice Questions

1 movement

2 Humerus — arm
Breast bone — chest
Jaw — head
Femur — leg
Collarbone — chest

3 The **outer** layer of bone is hard and strong.
The **inner** layer of bone is spongy but strong.

4 tendon, contract, force, move

Q5 (a)(i) The ribs are rigid and tough. This means they can protect delicate organs such as the lungs.

(ii) They move the ribs.

(b) It acts as a rigid frame for the rest of the body to hang off.

(c) joints

Q6 White blood cells are made in bone marrow, which is found in many bones. Some bones might start making abnormal white blood cells.

Pages 37-38 — Hopefully Helpful How Muscles Work Questions

Quick Fire Questions

Q1 It is the study of forces acting on the body.

Q2 The turning effect created when a force acts on something that has a pivot.

Q3 moment = force × perpendicular distance

Practice Questions

Q1 (a) Hamstrings and quadriceps should be circled.

(b) biceps and triceps

(c) Antagonistic muscles are pairs of muscles that work **against** each other. The muscles are attached to bones with **tendons**. This allows them to **pull** on the bone and move it. One muscle **pulls** the bone in one direction and the other pulls it in the **opposite** direction. In antagonistic muscle pairs, one muscle **contracts** while the other one relaxes. This causes movement at a joint.

Q2 (a) B

(b) the elbow

(c) moment = force × perpendicular distance
moment = 2 × 0.4 = **0.8** Nm

(d) 0.8 Nm
For the arm to hold the cake still, the moment of the muscle has to be the same as the moment of the cake.

(e) force = moment ÷ perpendicular distance
force = 0.8 ÷ 0.08 = **10** N

(f) It would move upwards.

(g) The force applied by his muscle will have increased because there is now a greater distance between the pivot and the cake.
When the distance between the pivot and cake increases, the moment of the cake increases (as to find the moment of the cake you would have to multiply the force by a bigger number). This means the moment of the muscle increases, so the muscle force also increases.

Answers

Pages 40-41 — Gorgeously Graceful Gas Exchange Questions

Quick Fire Questions

Q1 Small air sacs in the lungs where gas exchange takes place.

Q2 E.g. they are moist, they have a good blood supply and they have a large internal surface area.

Practice Questions

Q1 (a) oxygen, carbon dioxide

(b) The ribcage.

(c)

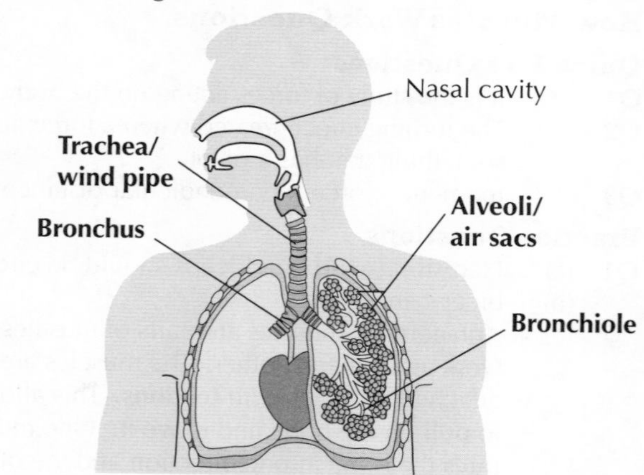

(d) It goes in through the mouth / nasal cavity, down the trachea, through the bronchi and the bronchioles to the alveoli, where gas exchange takes place.

(e) So that we can take in the oxygen we need for respiration and get rid of waste carbon dioxide.

(f) So it's easy for gases to diffuse between the lungs and the blood.

Q2 (a) Beneath the ribcage / under the lungs.

(b) Its movement helps to move air in and out of the lungs.

Q3 It allows gases to dissolve, so they can diffuse across cell membranes into the blood.

Q4 The breathing rate of someone with emphysema will probably be higher. Alveoli are the site of gas exchange so with fewer alveoli, less gas will be exchanged in each breath. They will have to take more breaths to make up for this.

Q5 When you breathe in, the concentration of oxygen is higher in your lungs than in your blood, so oxygen diffuses into your blood. The concentration of carbon dioxide in your lungs is lower than the concentration of carbon dioxide in your blood, so carbon dioxide diffuses out of the blood.

Pages 43-44 — Braggingly Brash Breathing Questions

Quick Fire Questions

Q1 It increases

Q2 It decreases

Q3 A machine for measuring lung volume.

Practice Questions

Q1 (a)(i) The balloons

(ii) The rubber sheet

(iii)The bell jar

(b) The volume inside the bell jar increases. This decreases the pressure inside the jar so that it is lower than outside. This causes air to rush in and inflate the balloons.

Q2 (a) 450 + 525 + 470 + 485 + 415 = 2345 ml
2354 ÷ 5 = **469** ml

(b) No. Different people have different lung volumes so you wouldn't expect them to get the same results.

Q3 When she blows into the balloon, her ribs move down and her diaphragm moves up. This decreases the volume of her chest cavity, increasing the pressure, which makes the air rush out of her lungs and into the balloon, causing the balloon to inflate.

Pages 46-47 — Extra Exotic Exercise, Asthma and Smoking Questions

Quick Fire Questions

Q1 Difficulty breathing, wheezing and a tight chest.

Q2 To trap dust and bacteria and stop them from entering the lungs.

Q3 It destroys air sacs/alveoli in the lungs. / It makes it difficult to breathe.

Q4 e.g. lung, throat and mouth

Practice Questions

Q1 (a) Tar covers and damages the cilia. This means the cilia cannot remove mucus properly, so mucus gets stuck in the airways, causing the person to cough more.

(b) They can cause (e.g. lung/throat/mouth) cancer.

(c) e.g. bronchitis

Q2 Your breathing becomes deeper and faster, to get more oxygen into the body. This is because when you exercise you need more oxygen so that you can respire more and release more energy.

Q3 (a) e.g. pet hairs / dust / smoke

(b) The muscles around his bronchioles contract. The lining of the airways becomes inflamed and fluids build up. All of these things narrow his airways.

(c) If his asthma is triggered, he can use his inhaler and the drugs it contains will open his airways again.

Q4 Her diaphragm and intercostal muscles may have become stronger, so her chest cavity opens up more when she breathes in. This would mean she could get more air in and out of her lungs in each breath. She may have developed more small blood vessels in her lungs and more alveoli. This would allow more gases to be exchanged in each breath. Both these changes would mean she would have to breathe less often.

Answers

ages 49-50 — Hugely Handy Human eproductive System Questions

uick Fire Questions

1 sperm
2 The lining of the uterus begins to build up.
3 day 14

ractice Questions

1

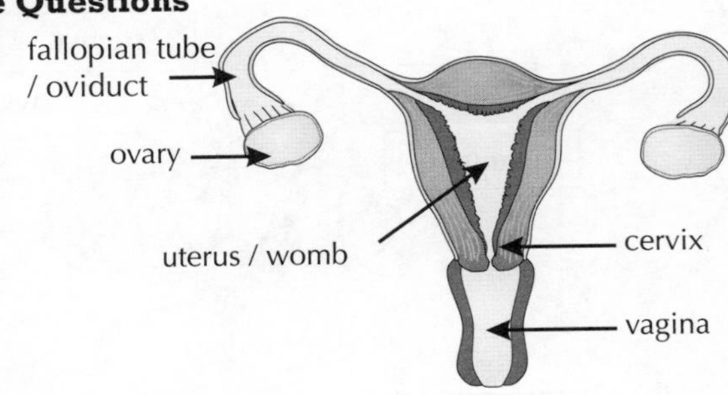

2 (a) C
(b) the sperm duct
(c) E. A testis.
(d) Semen is ejaculated out of the penis via structure D (the urethra) during sexual intercourse.

3 (a) About every 28 days.
(b) To get ready to receive an egg / for implantation.
(c) In the fallopian tube/oviduct.
(d) It passes out of the body (during a period).

4 An egg is released from an ovary on around day 14 of the menstrual cycle. Bleeding/a period starts on day 1 of the next cycle. A woman's menstrual cycle is 28 days long, so if the day that an egg is released is known, the next period should start 15 days later.

Pages 53-54 — Highly Helpful Having a Baby Questions

Quick Fire Questions

Q1 A foetus.
Q2 Because it reduces the amount of oxygen getting to the foetus.

Practice Questions

Q1 (a) ovulation
(b) implantation
(c) copulation

Q2 (a) From the mother's blood through the placenta and the umbilical cord.
(b) Any two from: e.g. it could cause it to have a low birth weight. / It could damage its brain / heart / liver / kidneys.

Q3 (a)(i) a zygote
(ii) 24 hours
(iii) Implantation — the embryo embeds itself into the wall of the uterus and the placenta starts to develop.
(b)(i) If her baby was born at this stage, it stands a fair chance of surviving.
(ii) A foetus.
(c) It allows the exchange of food, oxygen and waste between Parminder's blood and her foetus' blood.
(d) No. The uterus lining must be maintained during pregnancy.
Remember, a period is caused by the lining of the uterus breaking down.
(e) The walls of the uterus contract and the baby is pushed through the cervix and out of the vagina. The placenta passes out of the vagina after the baby.

Pages 56-57 — Definitely Dangerous (Health and) Drugs Questions

Quick Fire Questions

Q1 A drug taken for enjoyment, rather than as medicine.
Q2 Sensitivity and movement.
Q3 Regularly taking a drug to the point that it has a negative effect on your health or life in general.
Q4 e.g. cirrhosis/liver disease

Practice Questions

Q1 You should have circled:
All drugs affect life processes.
Drugs can damage your health.
Caffeine is a drug.

Q2

Type of drug	Effect on brain activity	Example of this type of drug
Stimulant	**Increases it**	**e.g. Methedrine / amphetamine (speed)**
Depressant	**Decreases it**	**e.g. alcohol / barbiturates**

Q3 (a) No. Even legal substances can be harmful if they are misused. If you inhale solvents they can damage your organs / cause you to suffocate / cause comas / heart attacks / death.
(b) Any two of: e.g. glue / paint / aerosols.

Q4 (a) Sensitivity, because each person tested had a slower reaction time after drinking alcohol. / Movement, as a person has to move to react.
(b) Person 3 because their reaction time increased the most.
(c) E.g. test each person at least three times and take an average. / Test more people.

Answers

Section 3 — Plants and Ecosystems

Pages 60-61 — Pleasantly Practical Plant Nutrition Questions

Quick Fire Questions

Q1 glucose
Q2 photosynthesis
Q3 Deliver water to the leaf cells and take away glucose.
Q4 They allow carbon dioxide to move easily between the leaf cells.

Practice Questions

Q1 (a) the roots
(b) photosynthesis
(c)(i) To make DNA and protein, and to grow.
(ii) Any two of: e.g. potassium / phosphorus / magnesium

Q2 (a)(i) photosynthesis
(ii) carbon dioxide + water $\xrightarrow[\text{chlorophyll}]{\text{sunlight}}$ glucose + oxygen
(b) Stomata. They let carbon dioxide diffuse into the leaf and oxygen diffuse out.
(c) So that there is a big surface area for absorbing the light needed for photosynthesis.

Q3 (a)(i) chlorophyll
(ii) magnesium
This is because magnesium is an important part of chlorophyll.
(b) Near the top of the leaf, because this is the part of the leaf that gets the most light.
(c) Because they don't get any light, so they don't photosynthesise.

Q4 (a) The level of carbon dioxide will decrease and the level of oxygen will increase. This is because as the plant photosynthesises it will use up carbon dioxide and produce oxygen.
(b) The level of carbon dioxide would increase and the level of oxygen would decrease. Without light the plant wouldn't be able to photosynthesise, but it would still be respiring. Respiration uses up oxygen and produces carbon dioxide.
The plant will still be respiring when it's in the light, but in the light the plant will take in more carbon dioxide for photosynthesis than it produces in respiration. Also, in the light, the oxygen produced by photosynthesis will outweigh the oxygen the plant uses up in respiration.

Pages 63-64 — Really Remarkable (Plant) Reproduction Questions

Quick Fire Questions

Q1 To enable them to reproduce.
Q2 That pollen is transferred from the stamen to the stigma of a flower on the same plant.
Q3 To attract insects for pollination.

Practice Questions

Q1 female, ovary, male, anther

Q2 (a) the flower
(b) Any two from: it is brightly coloured / scented / contains nectar/nectaries / has a sticky stigma.
(c) For pollination. / Because insects carry pollen between plants.

Q3 (a)

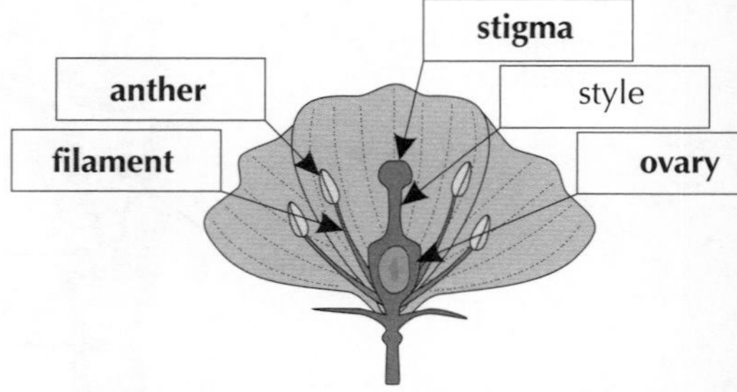

(b)

Part	Function
Sepal	**Protects the flower (in the bud)**
Petal	**Attracts insects**
Stamens	Helps in reproduction (male parts)
Carpels	Helps in reproduction (female parts)

Q4 (a) Pollen from another plant lands on its stigma.
(b) They might have small dull petals as they don't need to attract insects. They might have long filaments hanging the anthers outside the flower so a lot of pollen can be blown away. They mig also have feathery stigmas to catch pollen as it's blown past.
(c) self-pollination / plants pollinating themselves

Pages 67-68 — Fairly Fun Fertilisation and Seed Formation Questions

Quick Fire Questions

Q1 the embryo
Q2 the ovary
Q3 e.g. peas / gorse

Practice Questions

Q1 (a)

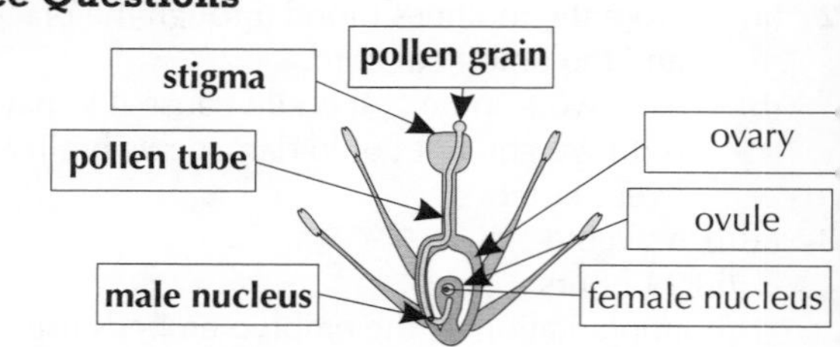

(b) A pollen tube grows down from the pollen grain through the style to the ovary. The nucleus of th male sex cell travels down the pollen tube.
(c) The male nucleus and female nucleus join.

Q2 (a) So that they can grow better, without too much competition from each other.
(b) They are often hard and heavy.

Answers

(c)(i) Because 'drop and roll' might not disperse seeds very far.

(ii) E.g. by carrying them on their coats. Some seeds are covered in hooks, so that they stick to animals' coats when they brush past. The seeds then drop off or are brushed off when the animal has moved away from the parent plant.

3 By wind. The light, feathery strands will help the seed to be carried by the wind.

4 (a)(i) A seed.

(ii) An ovule.

(b) This seed could be dispersed by animals. Animals would eat the fruit, including the stone/seed. This would then come out in the animals' droppings, away from the parent plant.
You can tell the seeds of this plant are dispersed by animals as it has a sugary fruit, which animals are attracted to.

ages 70-71 — Interesting Investigating eed Dispersal Questions

uick Fire Questions

1 At least three.

2 To make sure it is a fair test.

ractice Questions

1 (a)(i) The type of fruit. Whether or not the fan is on.

(ii) The distance travelled by the seed when the fruit is dropped.

(b) E.g. the height she drops the fruit from, the place she does the experiment, the distance from the fan to the fruit, the speed of the fan when it's switched on.

(c)

Trial Number	Distance Travelled (cm)			
	Seed A No Wind	Seed B No Wind	Seed A Wind	Seed B Wind
1	11	38	12	135
2	12	39	12	122
3	13	43	15	127
Average	**12**	40	**13**	128

(d) Yes, because seed A in no wind has the smallest range of results.
The range tells you how spread out the data is. If the range is small it suggests that the data is precise, as the results are all close to the mean. To find the range of a set of data, just take away the smallest data value from the biggest data value.

(e)

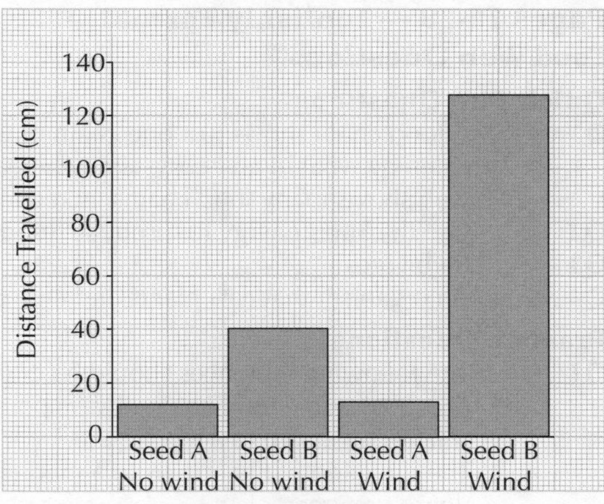

Make sure you pick a sensible scale for your bar chart (one that uses up at least half of the paper, and is easy to read). Label the axes clearly, and remember to put in the units.

(f) Seed B. It travels much further when the fan is on than when it is off. Seed A travels almost the same distance when the fan is on and when it is off, suggesting its dispersal doesn't depend on the wind.

Pages 73-74 — Definitely Delightful Dependence Questions

Quick Fire Questions

Q1 That organisms in an ecosystem need each other to survive.

Q2 the Sun

Q3 E.g. insects / bees / butterflies

Practice Questions

Q1 (a) Any two of: e.g. the gases in the air / the soil / the amount of light / the temperature.

(b) The flowers provide the butterflies with food/nectar. The butterflies pollinate the flowers.

(c) Almost all energy on Earth comes from the Sun. Plants capture the Sun's energy during photosynthesis. They use this energy to make organic molecules, which act as an energy store. This energy is passed on to animals when they eat plants. It is eventually passed to the snake when it eats other animals.

(d) It might decrease because there would be fewer plants producing oxygen through photosynthesis.

Q2 Honeybees are important for pollinating crops. If lots of the honeybees in Australia are killed by diseases from Varroa mites, not as many crops will be pollinated. This may mean that Australian farmers won't be able to produce as much food and so won't make as much money.

Answers

Pages 76-78 — Foolishly Formal Food Web Questions

Quick Fire Questions

Q1 A food chain shows just one chain of what is eaten by what in an ecosystem, whereas a food web shows many food chains linked together.

Q2 Use the Sun's energy to 'produce' food energy.

Q3 herbivores

Q4 An organism that eats plants and animals.

Practice Questions

Q1 (a) The following sentences should be circled:
The arrows in a food chain always point from a smaller organism to a bigger one.
The direction of the arrows in a food chain doesn't matter.

(b) a producer

Q2 (a) the beetle

(b) The shrew and the owl.

(c) the Sun

Q3 (a) seagull / seal

(b) herring / seagull / seal
Herring are both a secondary and a primary consumer in this ecosystem because they eat producers (plant plankton) and primary consumers (animal plankton and shrimp). Seals and seagulls are both secondary and tertiary consumers because they eat primary and secondary consumers (herring).

(c) herring

(d)(i) There are no shrimp for the herring to eat. The herring have less food, so their numbers decrease.

(ii) There are no shrimp to eat the plant plankton. There is more plant plankton for the animal plankton and the herring to eat, so more animal plankton (for the herring to eat) and more herring.

Q4 Because mercury that has been absorbed by plankton could accumulate/build up along the food chain. This could mean that humans get a very high dose of mercury if they eat too much swordfish.

Q5 (a)

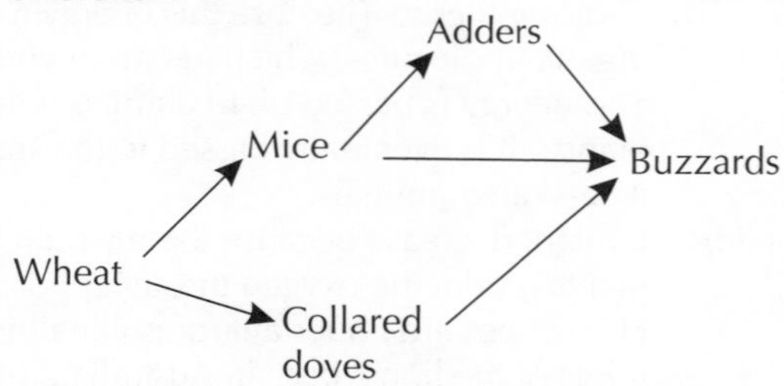

(b) The number of collared doves might increase as there are no mice to eat the wheat, so the collared doves get more food. The number of collared doves might decrease as there are fewer mice (and adders) for buzzards to eat, so the buzzards will eat more collared doves.

Section 4 — Inheritance, Variation and Survival

Pages 80-81 — Dangerously Diverting DNA Questions

Quick Fire Questions

Q1 DNA

Q2 46

Q3 They were the first scientists to build a model of DNA / showing what DNA looks like.

Practice Questions

Q1 (a) in the nucleus

(b) 23

(c) 2

Q2 The following sentences should be circled:
A gene is smaller than a chromosome.
Genes and chromosomes are both made of DN
A sperm cell contains 23 chromosomes.

Q3 (a) They collected data (including X-ray data) that Watson and Crick used to develop their model c DNA.

(b) DNA has a double helix structure. / DNA is mac of two chains wound together in a spiral.

Q4 (a) Because they have genes from both of their parents and genes control characteristics.

(b) heredity

Q5 (a) Yes. Having clubbed thumb is controlled by a gene, and hereditary characteristics are ones tha are passed on in the genes.

(b) It is possible that only one parent has the clubbe thumb version of the gene.
Remember, even though genes work in pairs one is usually dominant over the other. So it's possib that Emily only received one copy of the clubbe thumb version of the gene from her parents, but still ended up with the condition.

Pages 83-84 — Vastly Villainous Variation Questions

Quick Fire Questions

Q1 A difference between members of the same species.

Q2 environmental

Q3 e.g. height / weight / skin colour / intelligence / leaf area

Q4 e.g. blood group / the colour of a courgette

Practice Questions

Q1 (a) Different species have different genes. Genes control appearance.

(b) Because there may be differences in their genes/ inherited variation / Because of differences in their environment/environmental variation.

(c)(i) environmental, discontinuous

(ii) inherited, discontinuous

(iii) both, continuous

Answers

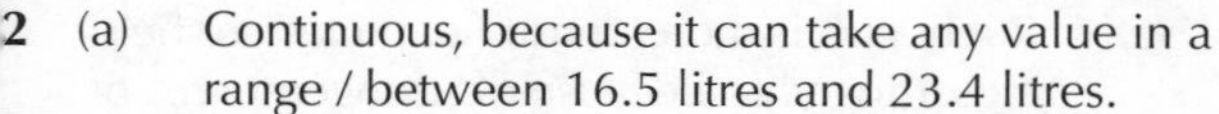

2 (a) Continuous, because it can take any value in a range / between 16.5 litres and 23.4 litres.

(b)

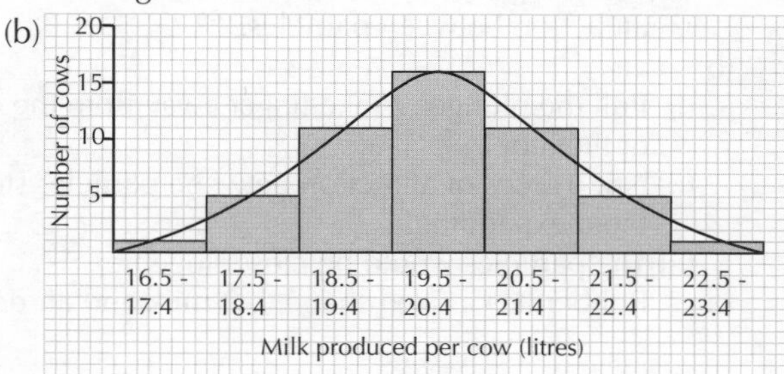

It's fine if you have drawn your graph using a different scale as long as it is sensible and easy to read. Just make sure you have plotted the bars correctly, labelled the axes, and that your curve is smooth and fits your graph.

ages 86-87 — Spectacular (Natural) Selection nd Survival Questions

uick Fire Questions

1 So it can survive and reproduce.
2 Any two from: e.g. food, water, shelter
3 natural selection

ractice Questions

1 (a) It will make the population decrease.
(b) After a few years, more than half of the frogs are very good at hiding.
(c) No. They may have to compete with organisms from other species.

2 (a) Slow antelopes get caught and eaten by cheetahs, so don't reproduce and don't pass on their genes to their offspring.
(b) Fast antelopes have survived and passed their genes on to the next generation. Slow antelopes have been eaten, and have not passed on their genes. This means the genes for running fast become more common in the population.
(c) The antelopes have become faster. Slower cheetahs will not be able to catch the faster antelopes, so will not survive and pass on their genes. Faster cheetahs will.
(d) E.g. they may have good eyesight / sharp teeth / sharp claws / a good sense of smell.

3 No. The mouse has no tail because of an accident, not because of its genes. It will still have the genes for a normal tail, so it will pass these genes on to its offspring (so its offspring will be born with tails).

Pages 90-91 — Extremely Exciting Extinction Questions

Quick Fire Questions

Q1 It may struggle to compete successfully / become endangered / become extinct.

Q2 False
Extinct means there are no members of a species left at all.

Q3 endangered (species)

Practice Questions

Q1 environment, compete, decrease

Q2 (a) It may become extinct / die out.
(b) The number of deer may increase.
(c)(i) gene
(ii) Scientists could use the sperm and egg cells to create new tiger embryos and increase the tiger population.

Q3 (a) They may become endangered / extinct.
(b) Some of the species found in the rainforests might be sources of useful products (like medicine, fuel or clothing). There may also be organisms in the rainforest that we haven't discovered yet that could provide us with useful products in the future.
(c) E.g. any two of: the environment getting hotter/ colder/wetter/drier / a new species being introduced to an area.

Q4 (a) A store of seeds/genes from different plants.
(b) If a plant becomes endangered/extinct in the wild, new plants can be grown from the seeds stored in the seed bank. This helps to ensure that there's a variety of different species on Earth.
(c) E.g. if species are preserved in the wild, they will still be able to affect the other organisms in the ecosystem that depend on them. This will not be the case if they are only preserved in seed banks. Also, there's no guarantee that an extinct species can successfully be brought back by using seed banks.

Answers

Chemistry

Section 1 — Classifying Materials

Page 8 — Surprisingly Savvy Solid, Liquid and Gas Questions

Quick Fire Questions

Q1 particles
Q2 gas
Q3 false

Practice Questions

Q1

Property	State of Matter
Easily compressed	Gas
Definite shape	Solid
No definite volume	Gas
Does not flow	Solid
High density	Solid
Medium density	Liquid

Q2 (a) Any two from, e.g. it has no definite volume. / It becomes the same shape as its container. / It has a low density. / It is easily squashed. / It flows easily.
(b) Any two from, e.g. it has a definite volume. / It matches the shape of its container. / It has a medium density. / It is not easily squashed. / It flows easily.

Pages 10-11 — Practically Perfect Particle Theory Questions

Quick Fire Questions

Q1 a solid
Q2 They spread out.

Practice Questions

Q1 (a) Particles in liquids are free to move but particles in solids are fixed.
(b) There's lots of free space between gas particles for them to move into when compressed. There isn't any free space between particles in liquids.
(c) Solids have lots of particles in a given volume, gases have very few particles in the same volume.
(d) Particles in liquids are held together, particles in gases are not.
Here, you have to say why one thing acts in a certain way and why another thing doesn't.

Q2 (a) It has no fixed shape.
(b) E.g. they have no regular arrangement/pattern. / They are able to move. / There's a weaker attraction between particles.

Q3 (a) Rubber. It is more dense / particles are held closer together because of stronger forces of attraction between particles.
(b) air
(c)(i) Pull the plunger. / Take finger away from the end of the tube.
(ii) No. Forces of attraction between particles stop them expanding.
(iii) The particles would be closer together.
(d) Rubber has a fixed shape, but milk and air do no

Pages 13-15 — Mostly Marvellous More Particle Theory Questions

Quick Fire Questions

Q1 E.g. Increasing the temperature, reducing the volume.
Q2 Particles spreading out.
Q3 The smell particles diffuse slowly through the air from an area of high concentration to an area of low concentration.

Practice Questions

Q1 (a) The oxygen particles are constantly moving. The pressure is created by the particles colliding with the walls of the tanks.
(b)(i) It would increase.
(ii) The same number of particles are in a smaller space, so collisions with the tank walls happen more often.
(c)(i) It would increase.
(ii) The particles have more energy, so they move faster, colliding more often and with more force with the sides of the tank.
(d)(i) It would have decreased.
(ii) There are fewer particles in the same space, so fewer collisions with the sides of the tank.

Q2 (a) Blue and white particles mixed evenly, e.g.

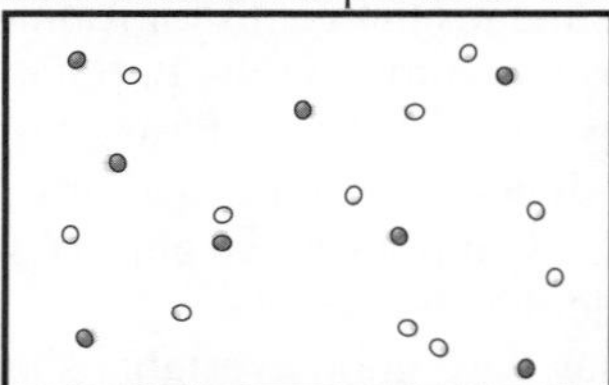

It doesn't matter if the particles aren't mixed exactly evenly — as long as it's roughly even.
(b) The particles gain more energy and move faster.
(c) It would diffuse more quickly. There are fewer air particles to collide with and slow down the perfume particles.

Q3 (a) The particles of A & B must diffuse through the tube before they meet & react.
(b) Gas A. Particles from A travel further than particles from B have by the time they meet, so A must have been moving faster.
If the gases were diffusing at the same speed, the ring of white powder would be in the middle of the tube.

Answers

ages 17-18 — Fairly Foxy hysical Changes Questions

uick Fire Questions

1 They gain more energy and move more.
2 subliming
3 liquid

ractice Questions

1 (a)(i) (ii) E.g.

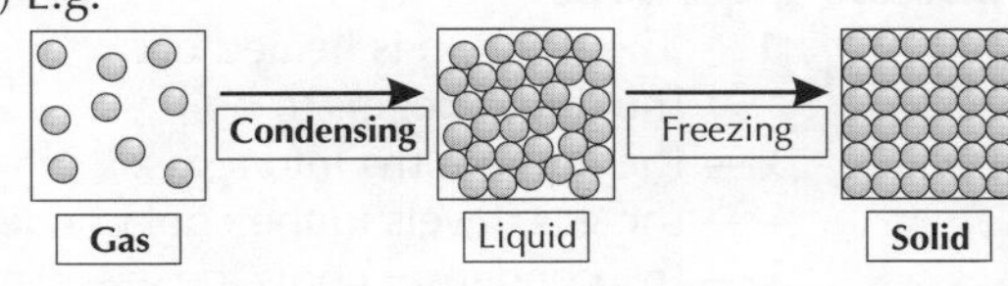

(b)(i) Particles move more slowly because they lose energy.
(ii) It increases. The particles are held more closely.
(c) G

2 (a) Time
(b)(i) B
(ii) E
(c) B, D
(d) 100 °C
(e) C
The water is still gaining energy in the flat bits of the graph, but it's being used to weaken the forces between the particles rather than raise the temperature.

age 20 — Amazingly Awesome toms (and Elements) Questions

uick Fire Question

1 The first modern scientist to try to explain atoms.

ractice Questions

1 (a) The following statements should be ticked:
All matter is made up of atoms.
There are different types of atom.
(b) E.g. Each element contains only one type of atom. Copper atoms are not the same as oxygen atoms. Each element has different properties. / Elements can be solids, liquids or gases.

2 O — oxygen, C — carbon, Fe — iron, Na — sodium, Cu — copper, Mg — magnesium

3 No. Each type of atom forms a different element. / Each element is made up of a different type of atom.

ages 22-23 — Perfectly Puzzling eriodic Table Questions

uick Fire Questions

1 In vertical columns called groups. Mendeleev.
2 1 and 2
3 0/the noble gases

Practice Questions

Q1 (a)(i) D
(ii) C
(iii)A
(iv)C
(b) 5
H and He are in period 1 — start counting down from there to work out the numbers of the other periods.
(c)(i) 3
(ii) metal

Q2 Potassium because it is the most reactive of the three metals.

Q3 Strontium will react with cold water because, e.g. calcium reacts with cold water and strontium is more reactive than calcium.

Pages 25-26 — Comically Clever Compound Questions

Quick Fire Questions

Q1 Two or more different atoms joined together.
Q2 Through chemical reactions.
Q3 H_2O
Q4 sulfuric acid

Practice Questions

Q1 One type of element — B and D.
One type of compound — F.
A mixture of elements — E.
A mixture of compounds — C.
A mixture of elements and compounds — A.

Q2 (a) Elements only contain one type of atom — water has two.
(b) Water contains more than one element/type of atom **and** these are chemically joined.

Q3 (a) **one** iron, **two** chlorine
(b) **one** zinc, **two** chlorine
(c) **one** hydrogen, **one** nitrogen, **three** oxygen
(d) **two** iron, **three** oxygen
(e) **one** aluminium, **three** chlorine
(f) **one** potassium, **one** manganese, **four** oxygen

Q4 (a) Sodium and chlorine react to produce the solid and chemical reactions produce compounds. The properties of the solid are totally different to those of sodium or chlorine (e.g. the solid can be eaten, but chlorine is poisonous).
(b) A lot of energy must be supplied to split the compound back up into its elements.

Page 28 — Naughty but Nice Naming Compounds Questions

Quick Fire Questions

Q1 "-ide"
Q2 Any three from: e.g. hydrogen (H_2) / nitrogen (N_2) / oxygen (O_2) / fluorine (F_2) / chlorine (Cl_2) / bromine (Br_2).

Answers

Practice Questions

Q1 (a)

Substance	Name	Chemical formula
A	hydrogen	H_2
B	carbon (di)oxide	CO_2
C	magnesium carbonate	$MgCO_3$ (also accept MgO_3C and CO_3Mg)

(b)(i) potassium + chlorine ⟶ **potassium chloride**
(ii) sodium + oxygen + carbon ⟶ **sodium carbonate**
(iii) copper + **sulfur** + **oxygen** ⟶ copper sulfate

Q2 (a) iron oxide
(b) carbon

Pages 30-31 — Mind-Bendingly Magnificent Mixtures Questions

Quick Fire Questions

Q1 A substance that is made up of only one type of element or only one type of compound. E.g. pure water.
Q2 A mixture
Q3 How much solute will dissolve in a solvent.
Q4 Soluble — the substance will dissolve
Insoluble — the substance will not dissolve

Practice Questions

Q1 (a) sea water, air, ink
(b) No. A mixture contains different substances.
Q2 (a) 100 + 10 = **110 g**
(b) solvent
(c) solute
(d) E.g. the bonds holding the salt particles together break. The salt particles then mix with the water by filling in the gaps between the water molecules.
(e) saturated
Q3 (a) As temperature increases, the amount of potassium iodide that will dissolve increases.
(b)(i) 140 g
(ii) 156 g
(c)

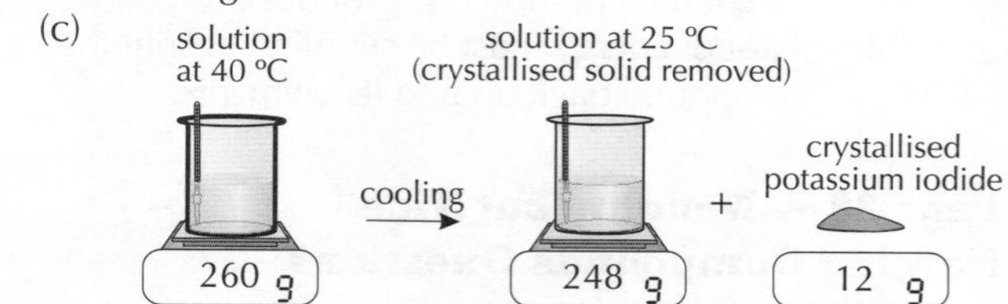

*To work out the total mass of the solution at 40 °C, you first need to find the mass of potassium iodide that will dissolve at this temperature from the graph (it's 160 g). Then add this figure to the mass of 100 cm³ of water (160 + 100 = **260 g**). Do the same thing to work out the total mass of the solution at 25 °C (148 + 100 = **248 g**). The difference between the two figures (260 – 248) is the mass of potassium iodide that has crystallised out of solution (**12 g**).*

Pages 35-37 — Simply Stunning Separating Mixtures Questions

Quick Fire Questions

Q1 crystallisation
Q2 a fractionating column
Q3 Pure water boils at 100 °C.
Pure ice melts at 0 °C.

Practice Questions

Q1 (1 — The solution is heated up.)
2 — The liquid begins to boil.
3 — The liquid turns into a gas.
4 — The gas travels to the cool condenser.
5 — The condenser cools the gas.
6 — The gas turns back into a liquid.
7 — The pure liquid is collected.

Q2 (a) To heat up the water and make it evaporate.
(b) Cool down the water vapour and turn it back to liquid water.
(c) The blue dyes have been left behind in the conical flask.
(d) E.g. heat it to boiling point. If it is pure, it will boil at exactly 100 °C.

Q3 (a) 1. C 2. A 3. B
(b)(i) A (ii) B
(c) Any one from: e.g. wear safety glasses to prevent glass getting into eyes. / Use spatula/container/spoon to transfer solid to avoid handling broken glass. / Wear gloves to avoid getting broken glass onto hands accidentally.

Q4 (a) It soaks up the wick and travels out from the filter paper's centre. It carries the inks through the paper, carrying some further than others. The more soluble inks travel further.
(b) E.g.

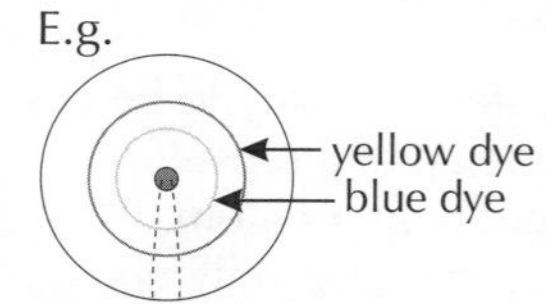

Q5 (a) fractional distillation
(b) Alcohol. The thermometer reading is 78 °C, the boiling point of alcohol. Water doesn't boil until 100 °C, so the vapour being condensed must be alcohol.
(c)(i) D
(ii) C. Alcohol is collected at stage B and water is collected during stage D.

Q6 (a) chromatography
(b) D. The spots are in the same position as those in the sample sweet.

Answers

ages 40-41 — Possibly Puzzling roperties of Metals Questions

uick Fire Questions

1 negatively-charged particles
2 smooth/shiny
3 They are sonorous.
4 It can be drawn into wires.

ractice Questions

1 (a) alloy
(b) Yes. It contains iron and nickel, which are magnetic.

2 (a) B, C, F
(b) A E.g. not all metals are magnetic. / Most metals are not magnetic. / Only certain metals are magnetic.
D Metals are not brittle. / Metals are malleable/ ductile.
E Metals are electrical conductors, meaning they allow electrical charges to pass through them.

3 (a) The atoms in metals can slide over each other.
(b) Metals have lots of particles tightly packed into a small volume.
(c) Hot particles vibrate strongly. They are closely packed so they pass vibrations on easily. Heat energy is also carried by free electrons.

ages 44-45 — Proudly Perfect roperties of Non-metals Questions

uick Fire Questions

1 heat and electricity
2 Any three from, e.g. oxygen, chlorine, helium, neon
3 E.g. sulfur, carbon

ractice Questions

1 (a) Xe, Br, O, Cl, B, I, Ne, S, F, C
(b) Any three of: xenon (Xe) / oxygen (O) / chlorine (Cl) / neon (Ne) / fluorine (F).

2 In most non-metals, the **forces** between the particles are **weak**. That's why non-metals **break** easily. They also wear away quickly because it's easy to **scrub** molecules off them.

3 (a) A, D, F
(b) B Most non-metal solids are brittle/shatter easily.
C Non-metals fill less than half of the Periodic Table.
E Some non-metals float in air.

4 (a) The forces which hold the particles together in non-metals are very weak.
(b) The atoms in non-metals are arranged so that electrons/negative charges can't move through them.
(c) Non-metals don't have smooth surfaces so they don't reflect light very well.

Pages 47-48 — Pretty Prickly Properties of Other Materials Questions

Quick Fire Questions

Q1 plastics
Q2 E.g. nylon / polythene / PVC
Q3 E.g. porcelain / glass / bone china

Practice Questions

Q1 Polymers are usually **insulators of heat and electricity.**
Ceramics are brittle, which means they are **not flexible.**
Ceramics can withstand **strong forces before they break.**
Polymers are made **by joining molecules together in chains.**
Fibreglass is made **by embedding glass fibres in plastic.**

Q2 (a) Fibreglass because, e.g. skis need to be light enough to carry and wear.
(b) Concrete because, e.g. the storeys of the car park will be heavy and concrete can support heavy things.
(c) Fibreglass because, e.g. the helmet needs to be light enough to wear, but strong so it won't break in a crash.

Q3 (a) E.g.

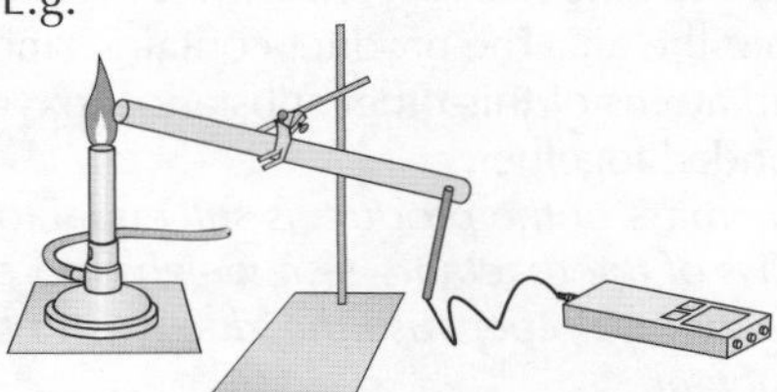

(b) E.g. heat one end of the rod in the Bunsen flame. Use the temperature sensor to measure the temperature at the other end of the rod. Record this temperature every 15 seconds for 2 minutes. Do the same for the other rod of material and compare the results.
The temperature at the other end of the rod will change the least for the material that's the better insulator.
(c) E.g. the length of the rod. / The temperature of the Bunsen burner. / The length of time she records the temperature changing for.
(d) E.g. Cherie might misread the temperature sensor. / Cherie might record the temperature changes for the wrong amount of time.
Random errors are usually caused by making a mistake while you're measuring.

Answers

Section 2 — Chemical Changes

Pages 50-51 — Coolly Calm Chemical Reactions Questions

Quick Fire Questions

Q1 No.

Q2 Any two from: e.g. temperature / colour / state

Practice Questions

Q1 The true sentences are: A, C, D

Q2 (a) H Cl

(b) O O

Q3 The missing words are:
27 g, reactants, the same as, product

Q4 (a) A (white) powder is formed. / The surface of the zinc becomes white.

(b)(i) tongs

(ii) Turn it to the yellow flame / turn it off.

(iii) The blue flame is hard to see, so you might not notice it, and end up burning yourself/your clothes/someone else.
Working safely is part of Working Scientifically. You should know how to use a Bunsen burner safely.

Q5 E.g. the zinc has reacted with something (oxygen) from the air. The product contains zinc atoms and atoms of this other substance (oxygen) bonded together.
The mass of the product is still equal to the total mass of the reactants — it weighs more than the zinc strip because the zinc wasn't the only reactant.

Pages 53-54 — Extra Exciting Examples (of Chemical Reactions) Questions

Quick Fire Questions

Q1 fuel, heat and oxygen

Q2 E.g. combustion/rusting.

Q3 When a substance breaks down into at least two other substances when heated.

Practice Questions

Q1 (a) methane + **oxygen** → **carbon dioxide** + **water** (+ energy)

(b) oxidation (reaction)

(c) It gives off energy/heat/light.

Q2 (a) thermal decomposition

(b) lead oxide
Remember thermal decomposition of a metal carbonate produces a metal oxide.

(c) carbon dioxide

(d) lead carbonate → lead oxide + carbon dioxide

Q3 (a) It ran out of oxygen.

(b) It had a (limited) supply of oxygen in the jar.

(c) E.g. as the (size/volume of the) beakers got bigger, the time it took for the candle to go out got longer.

(d) This happens because the bigger the beaker, the more oxygen is available to keep the candle alight.

(e) about 120 seconds / 2 minutes

Pages 56-57 — Quite Canny (More on) Chemical Reactions Questions

Quick Fire Questions

Q1 exothermic

Q2 A substance which speeds up a chemical reaction, without being changed or used up in th reaction itself.

Practice Questions

Q1 (a) Temperature has increased/changed. Solution/liquid has changed colour from blue to colourless. A new brown substance has been formed.

(b)(i) **exothermic** should be ticked

(ii) The temperature of the reaction mixture goes up, showing that the reaction gives out heat energy. An exothermic reaction gives out heat energy.

Q2 (a) It lowers the amount of energy needed.

(b)(i) volume of gas
The dependent variable is the effect you measure

(ii) catalyst
The independent variable is the thing you change

(iii) Any two of: e.g. temperature of the hydrogen peroxide (and catalyst) at the start of the reaction / volume of hydrogen peroxide used / concentration of hydrogen peroxide used / amount of catalyst used.

(c) Catalyst C because, e.g. it's the steepest curve / the curve levelled off the fastest / the volume of gas increased the fastest.

Pages 59-60 — Bizarrely Beautiful Balancing Equations Questions

Quick Fire Questions

Q1 On the left.

Q2 B

Q3 Because the number of atoms stays the same throughout the reaction.

Practice Questions

Q1 (a) copper + oxygen → copper oxide

(b) sodium + water → sodium hydroxide + hydrogen

Q2 (a) **sodium** + chlorine → sodium chloride

(b) $2\mathbf{Na} + Cl_2 \rightarrow \mathbf{2}NaCl$

Q3 $S + O_2 \rightarrow SO_2$

Q4 (a) $\mathbf{2}C + O_2 \rightarrow \mathbf{2}CO$

(b) $\mathbf{2}K + Br_2 \rightarrow \mathbf{2}KBr$

(c) $Mg + \mathbf{2}HCl \rightarrow MgCl_2 + H_2$

(d) $\mathbf{2}NaOH + H_2SO_4 \rightarrow Na_2SO_4 + \mathbf{2}H_2O$

(e) $\mathbf{2}Fe + \mathbf{3}Cl_2 \rightarrow \mathbf{2}FeCl_3$

Q5 $2Li + 2H_2O \rightarrow 2LiOH + H_2$

Q6 (a) 4
The balanced symbol equation shows that 1 molecule of nitrogen reacts with hydrogen to give 2 molecules of ammonia, so 2 molecules of nitrogen must give twice that (2 × 2 = 4).

(b) 9
The balanced symbol equation shows that 1 molecule of nitrogen reacts with 3 molecules of hydrogen, so 3 molecules of nitrogen must react with 3 times that amount of hydrogen (3 × 3 = 9).

Answers

ages 62-63 — Almost Amazing cids and Alkalis Questions

uick Fire Questions

1 pH 7
2 pH 0, red
3 It can show how strong an acid or alkali is.
4 Any three from: e.g. sodium hydroxide / ammonia / soap / washing up liquid.

ractice Questions

1 (a) red
(b) E.g. Wear safety goggles/gloves when handling the acid.

2

Substance	Colour in red cabbage indicator	Acid or Alkali?
Lemon juice	Red	**Acid**
Soapy bath water	Turquoise	**Alkali**
Vinegar	Red	**Acid**
Drain cleaner	Yellow	**Alkali**
Washing up liquid	Turquoise	**Alkali**
Lemonade	Red	**Acid**

3 (a) A chemical that changes colour when pH changes/to show whether a substance is an acid or an alkali.
(b)(i) The rain water was weakly acidic. The pure water was neutral. The sea water was weakly alkaline.
(ii) The pure water has pH 7, which is neutral. The rain water has a pH below but close to 7, making it a weak acid. The sea water has a pH above but close to 7, making it a weak alkali.
(c) She would have been able to say whether the samples were acidic or alkaline but not how strongly.
(d) No. Rainwater will have different amounts of pollutants in it at different times and places. The contents of sea-water will vary also from place to place.

ages 65-66 — Nearly Normal leutralisation Reactions Questions

uick Fire Questions

1 salt and water
2 sodium sulfate

ractice Questions

1 (a)(i) To make sure all the acid and alkali in the solution have reacted / none of the acid or alkali is left in the solution / he doesn't add too much acid.
(ii) green
(b)(i) sodium chloride
(ii) water
(iii) copper sulfate — sulfuric acid
sodium nitrate — nitric acid
zinc chloride — hydrochloric acid
(c) He wants to get larger crystals of salt.

2 (a)(i) mainly acidic
(ii) Mean pH =
5.5 + 6.5 + 7.0 + 4.5 + 8.0 + 6.0 = 37.5
37.5 ÷ 6 = **6.25**
(b) Do more tests at each hole and average the results.
(c) No, because, e.g. he doesn't know the pH of all the holes on the golf course, only the ones he's tested. / Some holes already have a suitable pH (6, 8, 17) and do not need liming. / Some holes are already alkaline and liming would make this worse (15).
(d) calcium hydroxide + sulfuric acid → calcium sulfate + water

Pages 68-69 — Roly Poly Reactivity Series (and Metal Extraction) Questions

Quick Fire Questions

Q1 sodium

Practice Questions

Q1 (a) 1. potassium 2. sodium 3. magnesium 4. carbon 5. iron 6. gold
(b) carbon
(c) E.g. try to burn each one in air — sodium will burn with a bright flame, iron will react slowly but will not have a flame. / Sodium will react more quickly than iron.
You could have compared them using any suitable reaction here.

Q2 (a)(i) reduction
(ii) iron oxide + carbon → iron + carbon dioxide
(iii) E.g. to make the reaction happen faster. / To give the reaction enough energy to start.
(b) It is more reactive than carbon, so cannot be extracted using (reduction by) carbon.
(c) Any two from: e.g. zinc, lead, copper

Q3 E.g. aluminium could not be easily extracted until electricity was invented, but we have been able to (use carbon to) extract iron for much longer.

Pages 71-72 — Ready-Made Reactions of Metals (with Acids) Questions

Quick Fire Questions

Q1 sodium
It's really worth learning that reactivity series — it comes in quite handy for questions like this.

Q2 E.g. copper / silver / gold

Q3 By holding a lit splint to the test tube — if you hear a squeaky pop, it shows the reaction is producing hydrogen.

Practice Questions

Q1 (a) Any two from: e.g. an equal amount of acid is used in each test tube. / An equal amount of metal is used in each test tube. / The test tubes are kept at the same temperature.
This question is asking you how Elena has made her experiment a fair test. So you need to think about the variables she should have controlled.
(b) C. Copper is less reactive than hydrogen so will not react. No bubbles appear in test tube C, so it is likely that no reaction is taking place.

Answers

(c) Bubbles show a reaction is taking place, so both metals are more reactive than hydrogen. There are more bubbles in test tube A, so this metal is more reactive than the metal in test tube B.

(d)(i) metal + acid ⟶ **salt** + **hydrogen**

(ii) A

(iii) magnesium + sulfuric acid → magnesium sulfate + hydrogen

Q2 (a)(i) It is less reactive than hydrogen/below hydrogen in the reactivity series and will not react.

(ii) These metals react too violently/dangerously with dilute acid.

(b) magnesium

(c) E.g. to make sure his results are repeatable / to increase the reproducibility of his results (by other scientists).

(d) Measure volume of gas/number of bubbles produced in a fixed time. The more gas there is/ the more bubbles there are, the more reactive the metal is. / Measure the time taken to produce a fixed volume of gas. The less time taken, the more reactive the metal is.

Page 74 — Really Rad Reactions of Oxides (with Acids) Questions

Quick Fire Questions

Q1 a metal and oxygen

Q2 the metal oxide solution

Practice Questions

Q1 (a) sodium + oxygen → sodium oxide

(b) It will neutralise the acid. / It will react with the acid to form a salt and water.

Q2 (a) sulfur + oxygen → sulfur dioxide

(b) It is less than 7.

Q3 (a) $2Mg + O_2 \rightarrow 2MgO$

(b)(i) neutralisation

(ii) magnesium sulfate

Pages 76-77 — Doubly Delightful Displacement Reactions Questions

Quick Fire Questions

Q1 Brown copper would coat the magnesium and the blue copper sulfate solution would go colourless. Because magnesium is more reactive than copper (so it would replace the copper in the solution).

Q2 Because the hydrogen from the acid is displaced by the metal from the alkali.

Practice Questions

Q1 (a) Any two of: e.g. the blue copper sulfate solution goes pale/colourless. / The nickel is coated with brown solid/copper. / There is a change in temperature.

(b) 1. nickel 2. copper 3. mercury 4. palladium

(c)(i) copper + mercury nitrate ⟶ **copper nitrate** + **mercury**

(ii) 3

(d)(i) Any nickel salt e.g. nickel chloride / nickel sulfat / nickel nitrate.

(ii) Chromium + nickel chloride* → chromium chloride* + nickel

** This could be chloride, sulfate or nitrate as in (*

Section 3 — The Earth and The Atmosphere

Page 79 — Easily Enlightening Earth's Structure Questions

Quick Fire Questions

Q1 crust

Q2 Tectonic plates are large pieces of the Earth's cru and the upper part of the mantle. They move ver slowly / a few centimetres per year.

Q3 earthquakes and volcanoes

Practice Questions

Q1 Quartz is a mineral that is found in the **rocks** that make up the Earth's crust. Quartz is made up of silicon dioxide, which is a **compound**. Silicon dioxide contains the **elements** silicon anc **oxygen**.

Q2 (a) Any two from: both have a crust. / Both have a mantle. / Both have a core.

(b) Mars' core is made of iron and sulfur. Earth's cor is made of iron and nickel.

(c) The scientists **observed** that boulders have rolled downhill. They came up with the **hypothesis** tha the boulders started to roll due to 'marsquakes'. In order for their theory to become accepted, the need to collect more **evidence** to support it.

Pages 82-83 — Rather Rocking Rock Types Questions

Quick Fire Questions

Q1 extrusive and intrusive

Q2 melted underground rock

Q3 sedimentary

Practice Questions

Q1 (a) Metamorphic rock is formed by a change in the structure of existing rock.

(b) pressure, time, heat

(c) E.g. marble

Q2 (a) E.g. granite is an intrusive igneous rock/forms underground, and weathering can only take plac on the surface.

(b)(i)

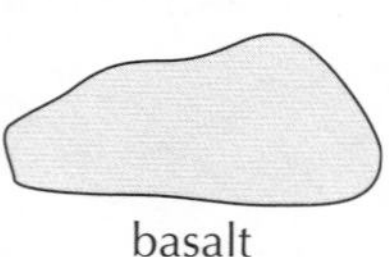

(ii) Basalt is extrusive, so it cools quickly and has small crystals. Granite is intrusive, so it cools slowly and has large crystals.

Answers

3 (a) 65 million years. Ammonites became extinct 65 million years ago, so the ammonite that Steven found must have died and been buried by sediment before then.
(b) The layer of rock with the fossil will be **younger** than the layer directly below it.
(c) E.g. dead matter and rock fragments/sediments fall to the bottom of the sea. Pressure squashes the water out and the sediment particles are cemented together by other minerals. Over millions of years, sedimentary rock is formed.

4 Any fossils in shale are destroyed by heat and pressure/the conditions when slate forms.

ages 85-86 — Rip-roaringly Raucous ock Cycle Questions

uick Fire Questions

1 E.g. onion skin weathering, freeze-thaw weathering
2 transportation
3 sedimentary

ractice Questions

1 (a) millions of years
(b), (c)

Q2 (a) sedimentary
(b) igneous

Page 88 — Reassuringly Restful Recycling Questions

Quick Fire Questions

Q1 E.g. energy, making plastics
Q2 Taking old, unwanted products and using the materials to make new stuff.

Practice Questions

Q1 E.g. energy usually comes from burning fossil fuels, which are limited resources. Energy is expensive, so using less energy saves money.

Q2 Sentence 2 is incorrect. It should be corrected to: e.g. recycling is efficient because it usually costs less than making new things from scratch.

Q3 (a) Something we use that we won't/can't get any more of once it's been used up.
(b) E.g. recycling some metals uses less energy than recycling others. / Recycling some metals saves more money than recycling others. / Recycling some metals produces less waste than recycling others.

Page 90 — Cheerily Charming Carbon Cycle Questions

Quick Fire Questions

Q1 Any two from: e.g. carbohydrates, fats, proteins
Q2 E.g. bacteria / fungi

Practice Questions

Q1 (a) B, D and E should be ticked.
(b) A should be rewritten as, e.g. photosynthesis is the process where plants take in carbon dioxide/ make glucose.
C should be rewritten as, e.g. only plants, algae and some bacteria can photosynthesise.

Q2 (a) Fossil fuels are made from the dead remains of plants and animals. Plants and animals contain carbon.
(b) E.g. through respiration

Page 92 — Actually All Right Atmosphere and Climate Questions

Quick Fire Questions

Q1 The gases that surround a planet.
Q2 Any three from, e.g. nitrogen / oxygen / carbon dioxide / water vapour / noble gases
Q3 E.g. burning fossil fuels, deforestation

Practice Questions

Q1 (a) The increase in the Earth's temperature.
(b) rising sea levels, failed crop harvests

Q2 (a) E.g. Global temperature has always varied. It started rising significantly about 1900 and is still rising.
(b) It comes from lots of separate experiments, which all show the same thing.
(c) Increased levels of greenhouse gases like carbon dioxide.

Answers

Physics

Section 1 — Energy and Matter

Pages 8-9 — Excessively Entertaining Energy Questions

Quick Fire Questions

Q1 When it is hot.

Q2 Energy is transferred from the elastic energy store of the rubber band to its kinetic energy store.

Q3 Energy is transferred from the gravitational potential energy store of the bobsled to its kinetic energy store (and a little to its thermal energy store).

Practice Questions

Q1

electrostatic	**two electric charges repelling each other**
gravitational potential	**a stationary roller coaster just before a big drop**
kinetic	**an athlete running a race**
magnetic	**a magnet attracting a pin**

Q2 (a) 'From the gravitational potential energy store of the block to the kinetic energy store of the block' should be ticked.

(b) 'From the chemical energy store of the block to the gravitational potential energy store of the block' should be ticked.

Q3 (a) Energy is transferred from the gravitational potential energy store of the diver to his kinetic energy store.

(b) Energy is transferred from the chemical energy store of the candles to their thermal energy store.

(c) Energy is transferred from the chemical energy store of the plane's fuel to the plane's kinetic energy store (and the engine's thermal energy store).

Don't forget that energy can be converted into more than one form.

Pages 11-12 — Extraordinarily Excellent Energy Questions

Quick Fire Questions

Q1 Joules (J)

Q2 Gravitational potential energy store

Q3 Energy transferred (J) = Force (N) × Distance (m)

Practice Questions

Q1 (a) 20 J

(b) 40 J

Q2 (a) In the spring's elastic energy store.

(b) Energy transferred = force (N) × distance (m)
= 15 × 0.2 = **3 J**

Q3 (a) Chemical energy store (of the battery)

(b) Any two from: kinetic energy store / gravitational potential energy store / thermal energy store.

(c) Energy transferred = force (N) × distance (m)
= 80 × 15 = **1200 J**

Q4 First find the energy transferred by the battery in car A: energy transferred = force (N) × distance (m
= 35 × 2000 = 70 000 J

Then find the distance that car B could cover with the same amount of energy:
70 000 J = 80 N × distance
distance = 70 000 J ÷ 80 N = **875 m**

You could do the second bit of this question by rearranging the formula and then putting the numbers in. If you used a different method, that's fine — as long as you got the final answer right.

Pages 14-15 — Horridly Helpful Heating Questions

Quick Fire Questions

Q1 From the hotter object to the cooler object.

Q2 thermal equilibrium

Q3 an insulator

Practice Questions

Q1 (a) Conduction

(b) Radiation

(c) Radiation

Q2 (a) Radiation

(b) No. All objects transfer energy to their surroundings by radiation.

Remember, all objects transfer energy by radiation— some just radiate more than others.

Q3 (a) Conduction

(b) Particles gaining energy at one end of the wire vibrate faster. Some of the energy of vibration is transferred to neighbouring particles, causing them to vibrate, and the energy spreads down the wire.

Q4 (a) E.g. Jess should put the same amount of water in each cup / she should make sure that the starting temperature of the water is the same in each cup.

(b) E.g. Jess should handle anything containing hot water very carefully/using heatproof gloves / she should put the hot cups on a heatproof mat.

(c) The metal cup, e.g. because metal is a conductor but plastic and cardboard are insulators. So the metal cup will transfer energy to the surroundings fastest.

Answers

ages 17-18 — Comparably Concise :onservation of Energy Questions

uick Fire Questions

1 Energy can never be created nor destroyed — it's only ever transferred from one store to another.

2 The rest of the energy has been wasted/transferred to non-useful stores of energy like the thermal energy store of the surroundings.

3 10 – 4 = **6 kJ**

ractice Questions

1 The following statements should be ticked:
Energy is only useful when it's transferred from one store to another.
Machines transfer input energy to useful output energy stores.

2 (a) No. Energy can't be created. It can only be transferred from one store to another.
She's actually transferring energy from a kinetic energy store to a thermal energy store.

(b) Machines like computers waste energy by heating their surroundings so rooms containing lots of computers are often warmer than rooms without them.

3 (a) E.g. Kettle A wastes less energy.

(b) Any two from: e.g. kettle A will be cheaper to run / will use less energy / will reduce the amount of fossil fuels used / will reduce pollution from electricity generation.

4 (a)(i) Useful energy = 100 – 75 = **25 J**
(ii) Input energy = 80 + 120 = **200 J**
(iii) Wasted energy = 400 – 80 = **320 J**

(b)(i) Kinetic energy store
(ii) Thermal energy store

ages 20-21 — Fantastically Elegant 'uel and Energy Questions

uick Fire Questions

1 We obtain energy from fuels by burning them.

2 Any two from: e.g. coal/oil/natural gas.

3 Sun ⟶ light ⟶ plants ⟶ photosynthesis ⟶ biomass (wood)

ractice Questions

1 (a) photosynthesis
(b) dead plants
(c) heats atmosphere, causes winds

2 (a) photosynthesis
(b)(i) Dead plant and animal remains get buried under layers of mud, rock and sand. They slowly decay over millions of years, turning into fossil fuels.
(ii) The fuel's chemical energy store
(c) E.g. wood and food.

3 The energy in the wind's kinetic energy store turns a turbine and a generator, generating electricity.

Pages 23-24 — Generally Joyful Questions on Generating Electricity

Quick Fire Questions

Q1 Non-renewable energy resources will run out one day. Renewable energy resources will never run out.

Q2 Fossil fuels are non-renewable/we're using up fossil fuels faster than they're being produced.

Practice Questions

Q1 (a) We are using up fossil fuels faster than they are being produced/fossil fuels are non-renewable, so one day they will run out. Burning less will mean they will last longer.

(b) Any two from: e.g. turning things off when you're not using them / driving cars with fuel-efficient engines / recycling more.
There are loads of things that you could have written here — anything sensible is fine.

(c) Any three from: e.g. wind power / biomass/plants / wave power / solar power.

Q2 (a) Advantage: e.g. you won't need to keep replacing the batteries / solar power is a renewable energy source so you will always be able to power the calculator / using solar power will save fossil fuels.
If the calculator wasn't solar powered, it would be running on batteries. Making batteries uses energy, which would probably come from burning fossil fuels.
Disadvantage: e.g. solar cells don't work when there's no light around/the calculator won't work in the dark.

(b) E.g. he could recycle the calculator / he could try to fix the calculator.

Q3 (a) E.g. coal (or any fossil fuel).

(b) 1 Letter **B** Name **Boiler**
2 Letter **C** Name **Turbine**
3 Letter **A** Name **Generator**

(c)(i) B
(ii) A

Pages 26-27 — Comfortingly Quaint Cost of Electricity Questions

Quick Fire Questions

Q1 Energy transferred (J) = power (W) × time (s)
Energy transferred (kWh) = power (kW) × time (h)

Q2 Electricity meters measure the amount of energy transferred in kWh.

Practice Questions

Q1 (a) The **energy** transferred by an appliance in kWh depends on its **power** in kilowatts and the **time** in **hours** that it is on for.

(b) One **kWh** is the amount of energy transferred by an appliance with a power of one **kilowatt** used for a time of one **hour**.

Q2 (a) 2 hours = 2 × 60 × 60 = 7200 seconds
Energy (J) = power (W) × time (s) = 40 × 7200
= **288 000 J**

(b) 40 W = 40 ÷ 1000 = 0.04 kW
Energy (kWh) = power (kW) × time (h)
= 0.04 × 2 = **0.08 kWh**

Answers

Q3 (a) Electricity at home = 27604.15 – 27431.65
= **172.5 kWh**
Electricity in the office = 61974.45 – 61844.95
= **129.5 kWh**
So she uses more electricity **at home**.
Just subtract the initial value on each meter from the final value.

(b) Cost at home:
Cost = Energy transferred (kWh) × price per kWh
= 172.5 × 10 = 1725p = **£17.25**
Cost in the office:
Cost = Energy transferred (kWh) × price per kWh
= 129.5 × 10 = 1295p = **£12.95**

Q4 2 hours 30 minutes = 2.5 hours
300 W = 0.3 kW
1000 W = 1 kW
100 W = 0.1 kW
Energy transferred = power (kW) × time (h)
Energy transferred by the TV
= 0.3 × 2.5 = **0.75 kWh**
Energy transferred by the heater
= 1 × 2.5 = **2.5 kWh**
Energy transferred by the lamp
= 0.1 × 2.5 = **0.25 kWh**
Total energy transferred = 0.75 + 2.5 + 0.25
= **3.5 kWh**
Cost = Energy transferred × price per kWh
= 3.5 × 10 = **35p**
As usual, if you worked this out a different way, that's fine — as long as you ended up with the right answer.

Page 29 — Politely Plucky Power and Energy Questions

Quick Fire Questions

Q1 The 2 kW heater.
The answer here is just the appliance with the higher power rating.

Q2 The 800 kJ stick of butter.

Practice Questions

Q1 (a) The **power** rating of an appliance, in watts, is the **energy** that it transfers per **second** when it's operating at its recommended **maximum** power.

(b) Energy in foods is measured in **kilojoules** (or kcals). You can compare the amount of energy found in different foods by looking at their **labels**.

Q2 (a) Runners Salty Shack. This bag contains more energy in total than the other one.

(b) E.g. the bag of Salty Shack is bigger / has a greater mass than the bag of Crumplies.

Q3 Energy transferred by the 2.5 kW heater:
Energy (kWh) = power (W) × time (s)
= 2.5 × 1.5 = 3.75 kWh
Time taken for the 1 kW heater to transfer 3.75 kWh of energy:
Time (h) = energy (kWh) ÷ power (kW)
= 3.75 ÷ 1 = **3.75 hours**

Pages 31-32 — Frightfully Fantastic Physical Changes Questions

Quick Fire Questions

Q1 In a physical change no actual reaction takes place and no new substances are made.

Q2 sublimation

Q3 gas

Q4 more dense

Practice Questions

Q1

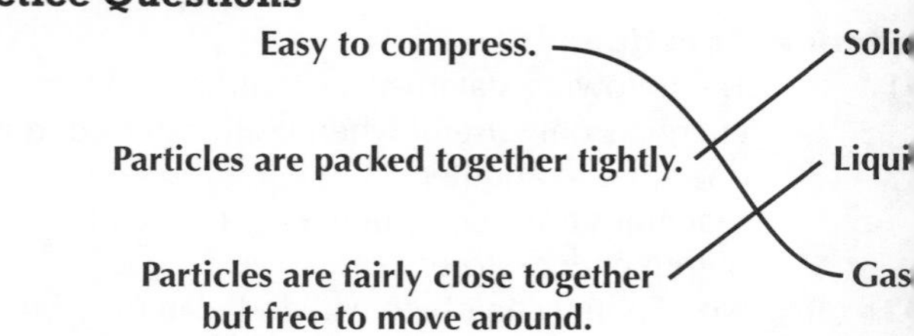

Q2 (a) A change of state, like a liquid becoming a gas, is **reversible**.

(b) When a physical change happens, the particles present at the end are **the same as** the particles present at the start.

(c) The total mass of substances before a physical change is **the same as** the total mass of substances after a physical change.

Q3

GAS LIQUID SOLID

Q4 (a) E.g. she should wear safety glasses/heatproof gloves / stand the apparatus on a heatproof mat.
There are lots of things you could write here — as long as your suggestion is sensible, you're fine.

(b) 10 g

(c) (i) The density should decrease.

(ii) No. Ice is different to most materials in that it becomes more dense when it melts.

Pages 34-35 — Positively Peachy Particle Movement Questions

Quick Fire Questions

Q1 Diffusion is when a substance moves from an area of high concentration to an area of low concentration.

Q2 The higher the temperature, the greater the movement of particles.

Practice Questions

Q1 The following statements should be ticked:
Air particles move around all the time.
This type of motion is called Brownian motion.
When air particles bump into dust particles, the dust particles move off in a different direction.

Answers

2 To start with, there are **lots** of smell particles where Sasha is. Gradually, they **spread** out. The smell **particles** have moved from where there are lots of them to where there are only a **few** of them. This process is called **diffusion**.

3 E.g. BEFORE AFTER

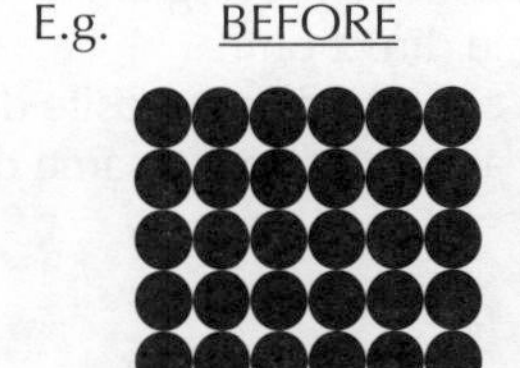

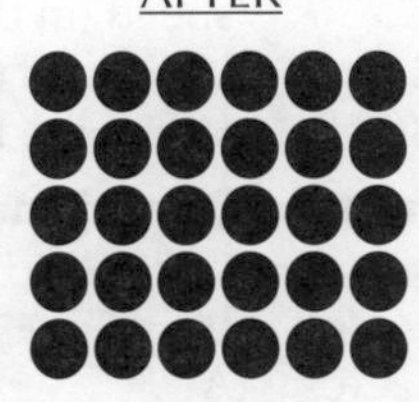

The second diagram should have bigger gaps between the particles, but it still have an ordered structure.

4 (a) More
(b) As the air warmed, its particles moved further apart causing it to expand and move out of the tube. The bubbles seen are the air escaping.
(c) As the air cooled its particles began to move slower and get closer together. The gas therefore took up less volume and the blue liquid moved up the tube to fill this gap.

ection 2 — Forces and Motion

ages 37-38 — Splendidly Spiffing peed Questions

uick Fire Questions

1 speed = distance ÷ time
2 E.g. metres per second (m/s), miles per hour (mph), kilometres per hour (km/h).

ractice Questions

1 402 m ÷ 22.8 s = **17.6 m/s**
2 38 cm ÷ 140 s = **0.27 cm/s**
3 (a) d = 700 m = 0.7 km. t = 15 mins = 0.25 hours.
s = d ÷ t
s = 0.7 km ÷ 0.25 hours = **2.8 km/h**
(b) d = 0.5 km. s = 0.1 km/min.
t = d ÷ s
t = 0.5 ÷ 0.1 = **5 minutes**
4 (a) d = 50 cm = 0.5 m. t = 5 s.
s = d ÷ t = 0.5 m ÷ 5 s = **0.1 m/s**
(b) d = 50 cm = 0.5 m. s = 1.0 m/s.
t = d ÷ s = 0.5 m ÷ 1.0 m/s = **0.5 s**
(c) d = 15 m. s = 2.5 m/s.
t = d ÷ s = 15 m ÷ 2.5 m/s = **6 s**
(d) s = 0.4 m/s. t = 23 s.
d = s × t = 0.4 m/s × 23 s = **9.2 m**

Pages 40-41 — More Surprisingly Spectacular Speed Questions

Quick Fire Questions

Q1 A steepening curve.
Q2 Add their speeds together.
Q3 Subtract the speed of the walker from the speed of the cyclist.

Practice Questions

Q1 (a) E.g. the vacuum cleaner starts moving and accelerates away from the charger.
(b) d = 4 m – 1 m = 3 m. t = 1 minute = 60 s
s = d ÷ t = 3 m ÷ 60 s = **0.05 m/s**
(c) Back towards the charger.
(d) Any two from:

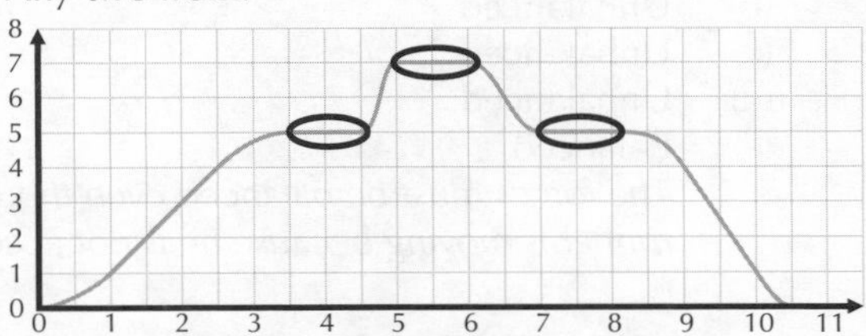

(e) Arrow pointing at steepest section of line, e.g.:

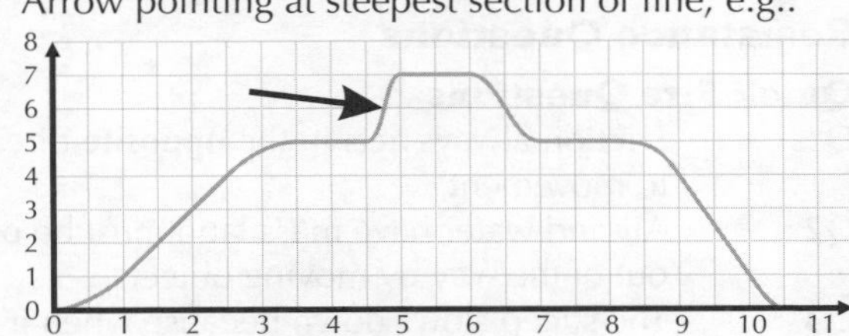

Q2 30 mph + 45 mph = **75 mph**
Q3 (a) 73 mph – 56 mph = **17 mph**
(b) E.g. t = d ÷ s
car's time = 25 miles ÷ 73 mph = 0.342 hours
0.342 × 60 = 20.55 minutes
bus's time = 25 miles ÷ 56 mph = 0.446 hours
0.446 × 60 = 26.79 minutes
car arrives = 26.79 – 20.55 = **6.24 minutes** sooner
You could do this calculation in other ways too, e.g by converting both speeds to miles per minute first. Any method that works is fine.

Pages 43-44 — Phenomenally Fabulous Force Questions

Quick Fire Questions

Q1 Forces are pushes or pulls that occur when two objects interact.
Q2 Forces are measured in newtons.
Q3 E.g. speed up or start moving, slow down or stop moving, change direction, turn, change shape.
Q4 Balanced forces produce no change in movement. Unbalanced forces change the speed and/or direction of moving objects.

Answers

Practice Questions

Q1 (a) Speed up.
(b) Slow down.
(c) Change direction.

Q2 (a) The strawberry will stay where it is.
(b) The strawberry will sink into the cream.

Q3 Forces act in **pairs** that **oppose** each other — an action force and a **reaction** force. Forces can't be seen, but the **effects** of a force can be seen. Objects don't always need to touch to interact. The **gravitational** pull between planets, forces between **magnets** and forces due to **static** electricity are all **non-contact** forces.

Q4 (a) Balanced
(b) Unbalanced
(c) Unbalanced
(d) Unbalanced
(e) Balanced
The forces must be balanced even though the runner is moving because he is not accelerating.

Pages 46-47 — Rather Rocking Resistance Questions

Quick Fire Questions

Q1 Friction always acts in the **opposite** direction to movement.

Q2 Air and water have mass, and must be pushed out of the way by moving objects.

Q3 The sheep slows down because when it opens its parachute the air resistance increases enormously (since there is a much larger area trying to cut through the air).

Practice Questions

Q1 (a) Any two from: e.g. it helps the tyres grip the road surface. / It allows the brakes to grip the wheels. / It holds together parts fixed by screws, nuts and bolts, etc. / It allows the rider to grip the bike.
(b) Any two from: e.g. energy is lost due to friction between moving parts. / Energy is lost in overcoming air resistance. / Air resistance limits the top speed of the bike.
(c) Streamlined.

Q2 (a) A frictional force which pushes against objects moving through air.
(b)(i) E.g. the skydiver begins to fall/accelerate downwards because the force of gravity/his weight pulls him down.
(ii) The air resistance increases as the skydiver's speed increases.
(c)(i) It increases a lot.
(ii) Air resistance and weight/gravity become equal/balanced, so no overall force is acting on the skydiver.
(d) The downward force of his weight is balanced by an equal upward force from the ground.

Pages 49-50 — Fiercely Fortifying Force Diagram Questions

Quick Fire Questions

Q1 The object will start to move.

Q2 The object will continue moving at the same speed (in the same direction).

Q3 When the forces are acting in opposite directions.

Q4 When the forces are acting in the same direction.

Practice Questions

Q1 (a) C
(b) B
(c) A

Q2 0.5 N
The mug is not moving, so the forces must be balanced and equal.

Q3 (a)

The arrows should be the same size.
(b) E.g. The car will accelerate because the forces are no longer balanced / the driving force is greater than the frictional force.

Q4 (a) Overall force
= 10 100 – 6350 – 4000 = **–250 N**
(b) E.g. the ship will slow down/move backwards, because the forces are unbalanced and the opposing forces are greater than the forward forces.

Pages 52-53 — Majestically Monstrous Moments Questions

Quick Fire Questions

Q1 A pivot is a point around which rotation can happen.

Q2 Moment = force × distance

Q3 They will be equal.

Practice Questions

Q1 (a)(i) Moment
(ii) newton metres / Nm
(b) M = F × d = 10 N × 0.25 m = **2.5 Nm**
(c) For the scales to balance the anticlockwise moment must also equal 2.5 Nm.
M = F × d
2.5 Nm = 4 N × d
d = 2.5 Nm ÷ 4 N = **0.625 m**
(d) Anticlockwise (weight):
M = F × d = 4 N × 0.1 m = 0.4 Nm
Clockwise (rice):
M = F × d
0.4 Nm = F × 0.25 m
F = 0.4 Nm ÷ 0.25 m = **1.6 N**

Q2 (a) Jade's moment:
M = f × d = 500 N × 2 m = **1000 Nm**
Ava's moment:
M = f × d = 400 N × 1 m = **400 Nm**
The see-saw would **tip on Jade's side.**

Answers

(b) Jade's moment:
M = f × d = 500 N × 1 m = **500 Nm**
Ava's moment:
M = f × d = 400 N × 1.25 m = **500 Nm**
The see-saw would **balance.**

3 (a) F = 4000 N d = 2 cm = 0.02 m
M = F × d = 4000 N × 0.02 m = **80 Nm**
Don't forget to change the cm into m to get the right units.

(b) Smaller. Jason's hand is further from the pivot (his elbow) than his arm muscles are. So to balance the moments, the force of the weight in his hand must be smaller than the force exerted by his arm muscles.

age 55 — Eerily Enchanting lasticity Questions

uick Fire Questions

1 They spring back to their original shape after the force has been removed.

2 Hooke's Law says that the extension of a spring is directly proportional to the force applied.

3 It means the force of the weight pushing down is equal to the force of the spring pushing up.

ractice Questions

1 (a) (i) & (a) (ii)

	Extension (cm)			
Weight (N)	Reading One	Reading Two	Reading Three	Mean
0.1	0.5	0.4	0.6	0.5
0.3	1.5	1.5	1.5	**1.5**
0.5	2.3	2.7	2.5	**2.5**
0.7	3.5	~~4.7~~	3.5	**3.5**
0.9	4.2	4.6	4.7	**4.5**

(b) The weight of the blocks.

(c)

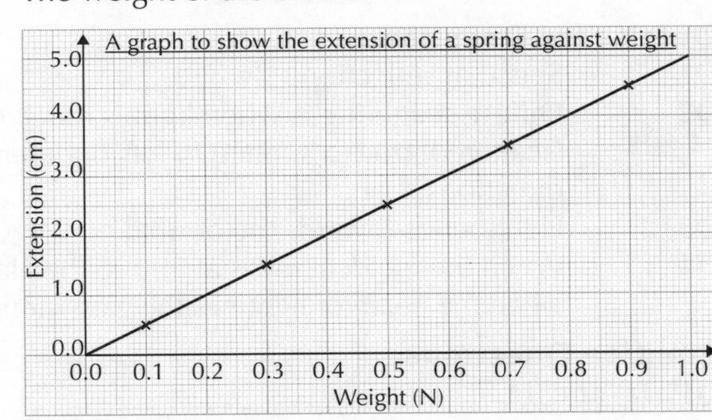

Remember to label both axes and give your graph a title.

(d) 2 cm (accept 1.8 cm to 2.2 cm)

Pages 57-58 — Peerlessly Practical Pressure Questions

Quick Fire Questions

Q1 pressure = force ÷ area

Q2 E.g. newtons per metre squared (N/m^2) and pascals (Pa)

Q3 Atmospheric pressure is higher at sea level because there is more atmosphere pressing down on you (so the pressure due to the weight of the atmosphere is greater).

Practice Questions

Q1 (a) E.g.

Weight 3000 N

Upthrust 3000 N

(b) The watercraft is experiencing an upwards force from the water (upthrust) that is equal to its weight. This stops it sinking.

Q2 (a)(i) F = 12 N. A = 0.00001 m^2.
P = F ÷ A
= 12 N ÷ 0.00001 m^2
= **1 200 000 N/m^2**

(ii) 1 200 000 Pa

(b) The head of the hammer has a much greater area than the point of the nail. So the same force is spread out over a larger area and the pressure on the wall is lower.

Q3 (a) 24 000 Pa. E.g. when Max lifts one foot off the floor, the area that his weight is acting over is halved. Pressure = force ÷ area, so halving the area must double the pressure on the floor.

(b) P = 12 000 Pa. A = 0.06 m^2.
F = P × A
= 12 000 Pa × 0.06 m^2
= **720 N**

Q4 As the packet gains height, the atmospheric pressure acting on it decreases, allowing the gases inside to expand. This causes the crisp packet to inflate.

Answers

Section 3 — Waves

Pages 60-61 — Weirdly Wonderful Water Wave Questions

Quick Fire Questions

Q1 Transverse

Q2 The crests combine briefly and their height doubles.

Practice Questions

Q1 (a) Water waves have undulations, or **up and down** movements.

(b) The undulations are **at right angles to** the direction of energy transfer.

(c) Reflection is when a wave hits a surface and its **direction** changes.

Q2

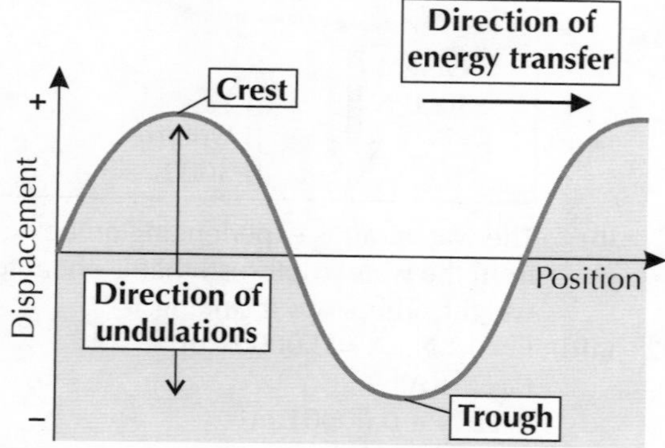

Q3 (a) Superposition

(b) When a crest meets a trough of the same size.

(c)(i)

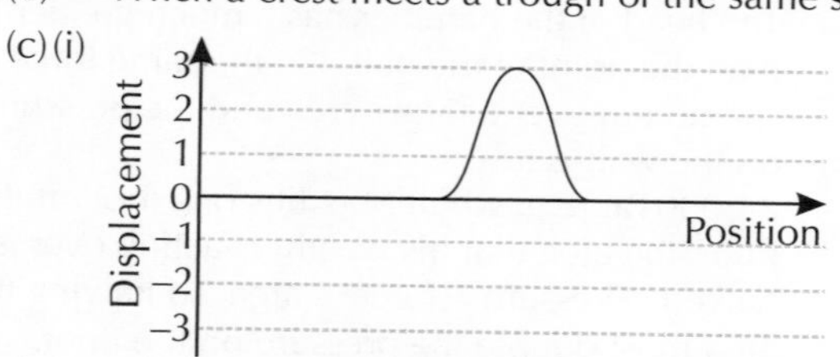

To find the combined displacement here, you just need to add the height of the two crests.

(ii)

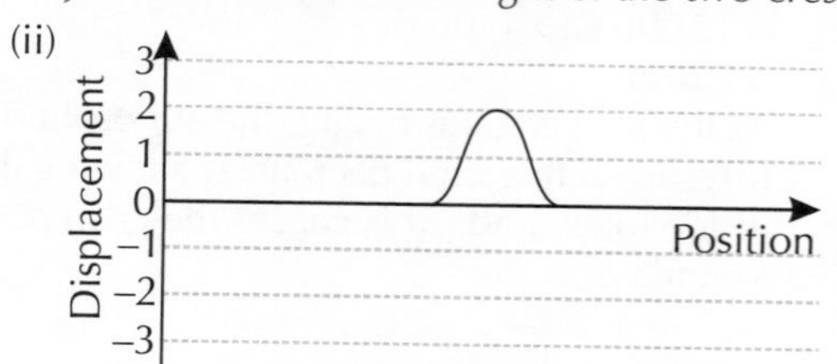

And to find the combined displacement for this one, you need to subtract the depth of the trough from the height of the crest.

Pages 63-64 — Lavishly Lovely Light Questions

Quick Fire Questions

Q1 E.g.

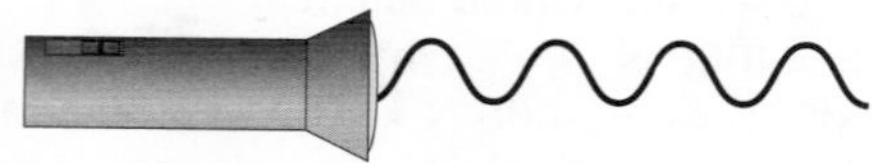

Don't worry too much about the torch — just make sure you've drawn the light wave as a transverse wave.

Q2 Light waves don't need particles to travel, so they can travel through a vacuum.

Q3 3×10^8 m/s

Practice Questions

Q1 Light travels fastest when it's travelling through **a vacuum**.
In this case, the speed of light is **a constant**.
When light travels through **a medium** it slows down.

Q2

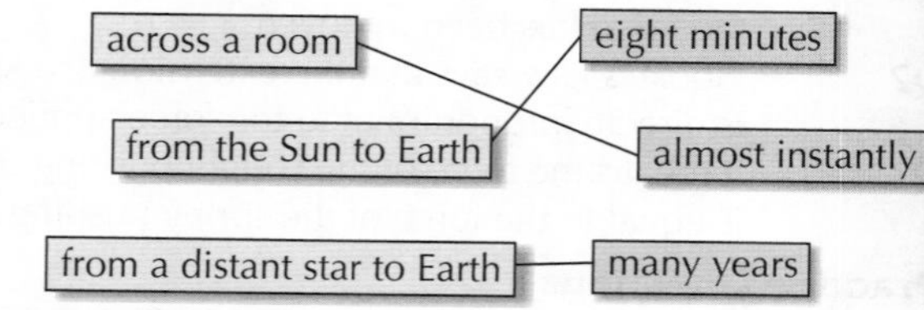

Q3 (a) transverse

(b)(i) The laser beam is reflected by the wall.

(ii) Waves can transfer energy — the laser beam is transferring energy to the wall.

(iii) E.g. light travels so fast that the laser beam will reach to the sensor almost instantly. If the sensor can only measure to the nearest hundredth of a second, it will make it look like the light is taking longer to reach the sensor than it really is / it will cause a big error in the measurement.

Pages 67-68 — Rightfully Riveting Reflection and Refraction Questions

Quick Fire Questions

Q1 Specular reflection

Q2 Diffuse scattering is when light is reflected (scattered) from a surface in lots of different directions.

Q3 Light bends towards the normal.

Q4 When the incident ray is at 90 ° to the glass / when the beam of light hits the glass straight on.

Practice Questions

Q1 (a) and (b)

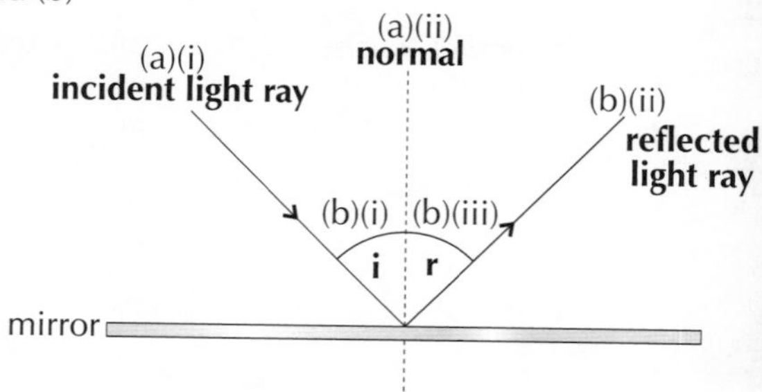

For the reflected ray to be drawn correctly, angle r must be the same as angle i.

Answers

(c)(i) angle of incidence = angle of reflection / angle i = angle r / the angle of incidence is equal to the angle of reflection.
(ii) The mirror has a smooth, shiny surface.
(iii) When light falls on an object with a surface that is rough and dull / not smooth and shiny.

2 (a) E.g. the angle of the incident ray / the position of the light source / the light source/colour of light used.
(b) When the light ray went from air to water, it bent towards the normal.
(c) E.g. the light ray bends more when it goes from air to glass than it does when it goes from air to water, so glass must be more dense than water.
(d) The refracted ray should be bent towards the normal. E.g.:

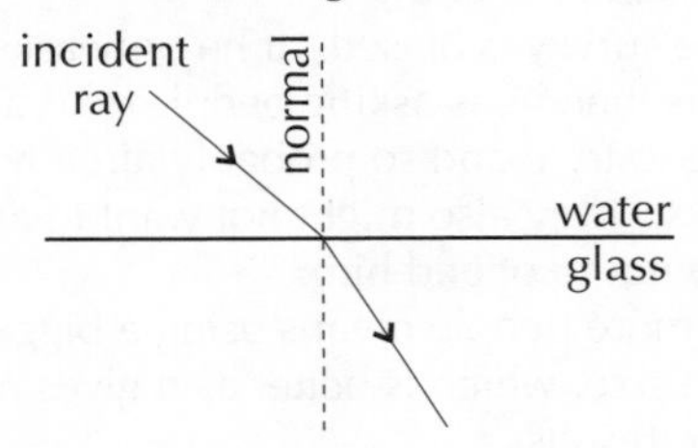

ages 70-71 — Strangely Satisfactory uestions on How We See

uick Fire Questions

1 A convex lens causes rays of light to converge towards a focus / focuses light rays.
2 The iris controls the amount of light entering the eye.
3 The digital image sensor.

ractice Questions

1 (a) E.g.

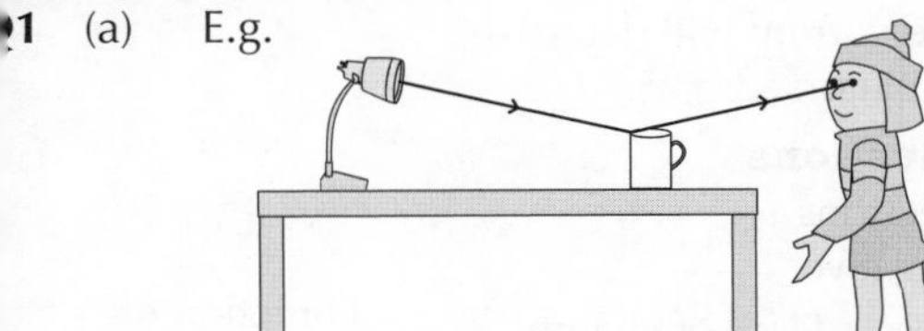

Remember that light travels in straight lines — so use a ruler to draw light rays in your answers.

(b) Light from the table lamp reflects off the mug and into Charmaine's eyes.

2 (a)

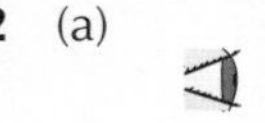
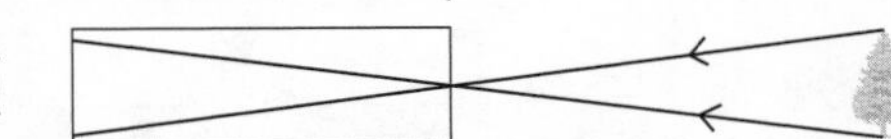

(b) The light rays cross over inside the camera, reversing the image.

3 (a) the retina
(b) When energy is absorbed by the retina it causes chemical and electrical changes in cells. (This causes electrical signals to be sent to the brain.)
(c)(i) The cornea and the lens.
(ii)

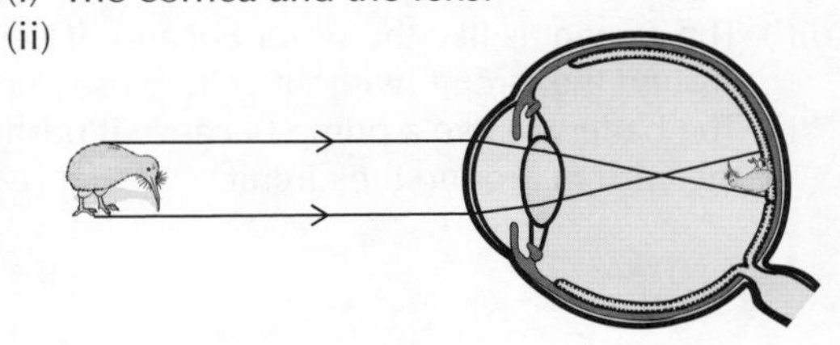

Pages 73-74 — Cautiously Cool Colour Questions

Quick Fire Questions

Q1 Red, orange, yellow, green, blue, indigo, violet
Q2 A green filter absorbs red light / only allows green light to pass through.
Q3 Black
Blue jeans only reflect blue light, so they'll look black in anything except blue or white light.

Practice Questions

Q1 (a)(i) spectrum
(ii) dispersal
(b)(i) red
(ii) violet
(c)(i) The white light entering the prism contains **all** of the colours of the rainbow.
(ii) The light is split because each colour has a different **frequency**.
(iii) The colour of light with the lowest frequency is **red**.

Q2 (a) **A**: Red. The flower reflects only red light, which passes through the filter to Eric's eye.
B: Red. The flower reflects the red light, Which passes through the filter to Eric's eye.
C: Black. There is no red light for the flower to reflect/the flower cannot reflect the blue light, so it looks black.
D: Black. The flower reflects red light, which passes through the magenta filter but is absorbed by the blue filter.
(b) Black. The leaves only reflect green light. In B, C and D there is no green light for the leaves to reflect. In A the green light reflected by the leaves will be absorbed by the filter.

Pages 76-77 — Sonorously Sensational Sound Questions

Quick Fire Questions

Q1 Longitudinal waves
Q2 Sound travels fastest in a solid.
Q3 Hertz

Practice Questions

Q1 (a) Light waves can travel through a vacuum but sound waves cannot.
(b) The sound vibrations of Zach's voice pass through the air in his helmet, through the touching helmets, through the air in Joel's helmet, to Joel's ear.

Q2 (a)(i) An echo.
(ii) They were reflected from the cave walls.
(b) The vibrations take time to travel to the cave walls and back again.
(c) The cave walls have absorbed some of the sound.

Answers

Q3 (a)(i) The number of complete waves that pass a point in one second / the number of vibrations per second.

(ii) The higher the frequency of a noise, the higher it sounds/the higher pitched it is.
If you write this the other way round (the lower the frequency, the lower the pitch) that's fine.

(b) 1 A road drill,
2 A car engine,
3 A dentist's drill,
4 A scream.

Page 79 — Healthily Hearty Hearing Questions

Quick Fire Questions

Q1 Your auditory range is the range of frequencies that you can hear.

Q2 20 - 20 000 Hz

Q3 E.g. dogs / bats / dolphins.

Practice Questions

Q1 (a)

(b) The vibrations are passed from Lila's vocal chords to the air, to Heather's ear drum, then to her ear bones and on to her cochlea. Hairs in her cochlea vibrate, sending a message to the brain via the auditory nerve.

Q2 (a) E.g. Matthew could start by playing sounds with frequencies much higher than 20 000 Hz. Then he could play sounds of gradually decreasing frequency until the person raises their hand.
The typical auditory range of humans is 20 to 20 000 Hz, but some people might be able to hear sounds higher than 20 000 Hz — that's why Matthew should make sure the starting frequency is above this.

(b) Any two from: e.g. the loudspeaker should be set at the same volume. / They should be sat at the same distance from the loudspeaker. / The increases or decreases in frequency should be the same size. / They should have the same number of attempts at hearing a frequency.

Pages 81-82 — Endearingly Wondrous Energy and Wave Questions

Quick Fire Questions

Q1 Sound waves transfer information through vibrations between particles / pressure changes.

Q2 The diaphragm

Q3 Ultrasound is sound with a higher pitch than the normal auditory range of humans / sound with a frequency over 20 000 Hz.

Q4 The false teeth are placed in a special bath filled with water. High-pressure ultrasound waves cause bubbles to form in cavities, knocking off any dirt.

Practice Questions

Q1 Sound waves transfer **energy** and information through **pressure** changes. Microphones detect this information through vibrations in a **diaphragm**. After the microphone has detected the information, it converts it to **electrical** signal

Q2 (a) The electrical signals cause a diaphragm in the loudspeaker to vibrate, which causes air to vibrate, producing sound waves.

(b) Ultrasound pressure waves can transfer energy through matter, so they can reach hard-to-acces areas inside the body.

(c)(i) E.g. the survey is biased. If he only asks his patients then he is asking people who are alread willing to try it and so probably already believe it works. They also might not want to answer 'no' so not to offend him.

(ii) Using more people means using a bigger sample size, which is better as it gives more reliable results.
Using a bigger sample size reduces the effect that any anomalous (odd) results have on the overall result.

Section 4 — Electricity and Magnetism

Pages 84-85 — Seriously Scintillating Circuit Questions

Quick Fire Questions

Q1 A battery

Q2 The current will decrease.

Q3 Insulators

Practice Questions

Q1 (a) Electrons
(b) Negative

Q2 (a)

You could have put your arrows anywhere on the diagram, as long as they're pointing in the right direction.

(b) Current would stop flowing if there was a break in the circuit / the bulb would go out.

(c) Current would increase.

(d)(i) The current is like the water because it flows around the circuit (without getting used up).

(ii) The battery is like a pump because it pushes the current around the circuit.

Answers

A: resistance = p.d. ÷ current = 2.4 ÷ 0.00024
= 10 000 Ω
A is an insulator.
B: resistance = p.d. ÷ current = 2.4 ÷ 16 = **0.14 Ω**
B is a conductor.
C: resistance = p.d. ÷ current = 2.4 ÷ 10 = **0.24 Ω**
C is a conductor.

ge 87 — Curious Current and torious Voltage Questions
ck Fire Questions
The potential difference the battery supplies.
To show the maximum potential difference you can safely put across them.

ctice Questions
(a) Current is measured in **amps** using an **ammeter**.
(b) Potential difference is measured in **volts** using a **voltmeter**.

(a)

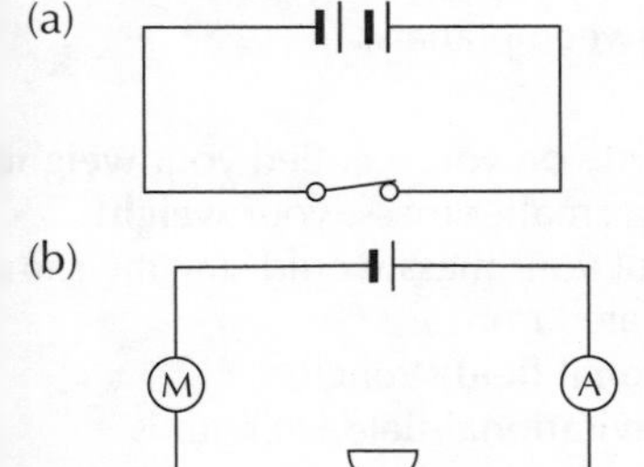

(b)

ges 90-91 — Splendid Series and fect Parallel Circuit Questions
ck Fire Questions
The current is the same through each component.
The potential difference of the cell (or battery).
The current flowing through the cell / the total current of the circuit.
The potential difference is the same across each branch.

ctice Questions
(a) A parallel circuit is one where the current has a choice of routes / branches to flow along.
(b)(i) A_1
(ii) A_2
(a) A series circuit is one where there is only one route for the current to flow.
(b)

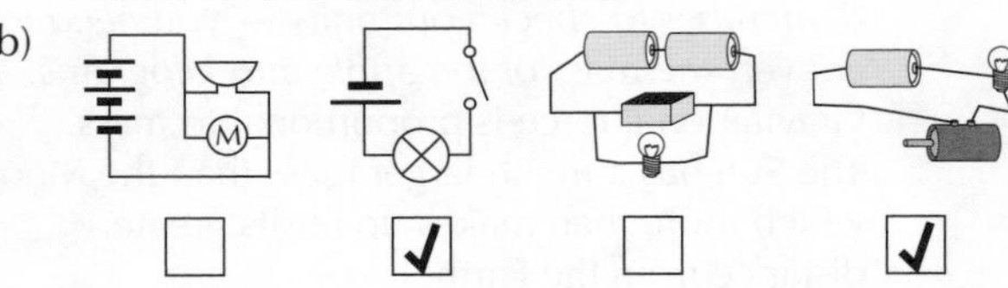

(a) 10.5 A
This is just the same as A_1.
(b) $V_3 = 18 - 5.5 - 7 = 5.5$ V
(a)

Ammeter	1	2	3	4	5
Reading (A)	8	2	5	**1**	**8**

A_5 is the same as A_1.
A_2, A_3 and A_4 add up to A_1 or A_5 $(2 + 5 + A_4 = 8)$.

(b) Ammeter 1 is faulty. The readings on A_1 and A_5 should both be the sum of the readings on A_2, A_3 and A_4 (21 A), but A_1 only measures 13 A.

Q5

Switches				Bulbs		
A	B	C	D	1	2	3
open	closed	closed	closed	off	on	on
closed	open	closed	closed	**on**	**off**	**off**
closed	closed	open	closed	**on**	**off**	**on**
closed	closed	closed	open	**on**	**on**	**off**
closed	closed	open	open	**on**	**off**	**off**
closed	open	open	closed	**on**	**off**	**off**
closed	closed	closed	closed	**on**	**on**	**on**

Page 93 — Stupendously Satisfying Static Electricity Questions
Quick Fire Questions
Q1 Negative
Q2 Negative charges

Practice Questions
Q1 (a) The balloon is positively charged.
(b) The cloth is negatively charged.
(c) When the cloth and the balloon were rubbed together, electrons were scraped off the balloon and left on the cloth, giving the balloon a positive charge and the cloth a negative charge.
(d) No.
Q2 (a) Charged objects have an electric **field** around them.
(b) This is a region where other charged objects feel a **force** without needing to come in **contact**.
(c) A negatively charged object attracts objects with a **positive** charge and repels objects with a **negative** charge.

Page 95-96 — Magically Magnificent Magnet Questions
Quick Fire Questions
Q1 From the North pole to the South pole.
Q2 They would repel each other.
Q3 A compass will align itself to the Earth's magnetic field / point to the Earth's magnetic North pole.

Practice Questions
Q1 (a) A magnetic field is a region where magnetic materials experience a force.
(b)(i) It will point from north to south along the field lines.
(ii)

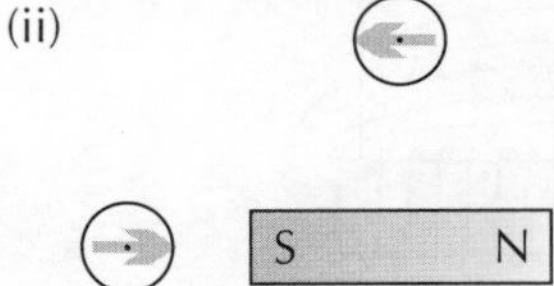

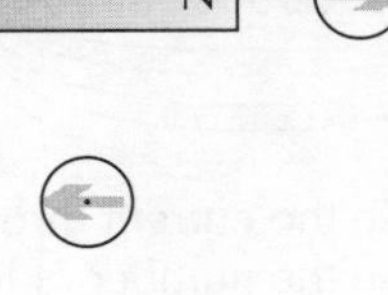

Answers

(c) Scatter iron filings around a bar magnet. They will align along the field lines.

(d)

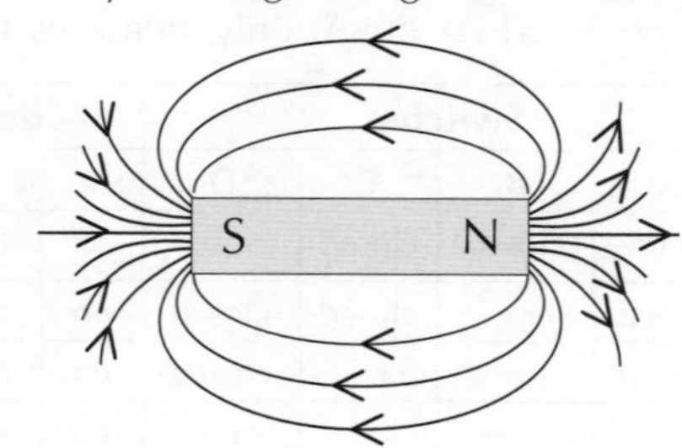

Q2 C is not a magnet. E.g. a piece of steel is always attracted to magnets. A magnet can be attracted or repelled by other magnets. A and B sometimes repel each other, but C is always attracted to A and B.

Pages 98-99 — Excitingly Erudite Electromagnet Questions

Quick Fire Questions

Q1 A magnet made from a current-carrying wire / solenoid.

Q2 An electric motor is made from a loop of coiled wire in a magnetic field. When current flows through the wire, a magnetic field forms around the wire. Each side of the loop then feels a force from the magnetic field that was already there. The current in each side of the wire flows in opposite directions, so one side pushes up and the other side pushes down. This causes the wire loop to turn.

Practice Questions

Q1 (a) E.g. Rajesh could make a solenoid. A solenoid is a long coil of wire. It can be made into an electromagnet by connecting it to a circuit and running a current through it, like this:

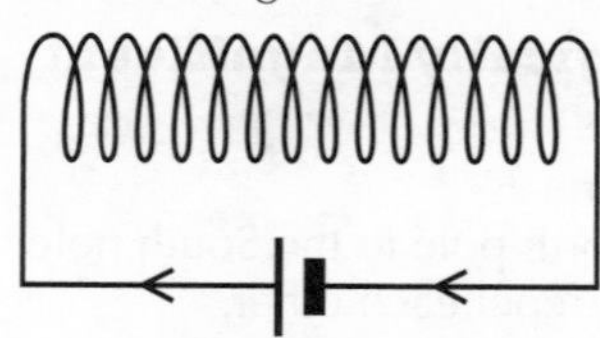

(b) Steel stays magnetised after the current through the wire has been turned off. So he would not be able to turn the magnet on and off again.

Q2 (a)(i) A long coil of wire.

(ii) An electromagnet

(b)

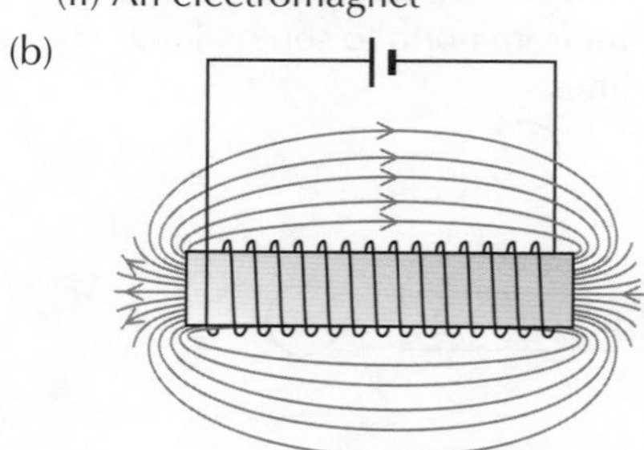

(c) 1. Increase the current through the wire.
2. Increase the number of loops in the solenoid.
3. Replace the cardboard tube with a soft iron core.

(d) Electromagnets require electricity, which can be dangerous.

(e) Any three from: e.g. don't mix water and any electrical devices / don't touch bare or frayed electrical wires / don't put too much potential difference across components which can't handle it / turn electrical devices off when not using them / check if a component is hot before touching by placing a hand near it.

Section 5 — The Earth and Beyond

Pages 101-102 — Gratifyingly Great Gravity Questions

Quick Fire Questions

Q1 Gravity attracts anything with a mass.

Q2 The Moon stays in orbit because the Earth and Moon are attracted by gravity.

Q3 Weight is caused by the pull of gravity, which varies between planets.

Practice Questions

Q1 (a) The force of gravity on you is called your **weight**

(b) If the Earth had a smaller mass, your **weight** would be less but your **mass** would stay the same

(c) Weight is calculated from **mass × gravitational field** strength.

(d) On Earth the **gravitational field** strength is about **ten** N/kg.

Q2 The astronauts have less weight because the Moon's gravity is weaker than Earth's.

Q3

Object	Body	Gravitational Field Strength (N/kg)	Weight (N)
Peter (mass = 60 kg)	Mercury	3.7	60 × 3.7 = **222**
1.5 kg bag of flour	Jupiter	25	1.5 × 25 = **37.5**
1000 kg car	Uranus	8.7	1000 × 8.7 = **8700**
100 g apple	Pluto	0.6	0.1 × 0.6 = **0.06**

Remember to check your units — you need to convert the mass of the apple into kilograms.

Q4 (a) Gravitational force is proportional to mass. The Sun has a much larger mass than the Moon, which more than makes up for its greater distance from the Earth.

(b) About 10 N/kg

(c) The gravitational field strength on the Sun would be greater than on Earth because the Sun has a much larger mass.

Answers

ages 104-105 — Suspiciously Sublime ın and Star Questions

uick Fire Questions

1 A star is an extremely massive ball of hot gas, held together by gravity, that gives out heat and light.

2 Proxima Centauri.

3 A light year is the distance that light travels in one year.

ractice Questions

1 (1) Planet Earth,
(2) the Sun,
(3) a galaxy,
(4) the Universe.

2 (a) A collection of many stars.
(b) The Milky Way.
(c) 'Billions' should be circled.

3 (a) The Sun is the star at the centre of our **Solar** System.
(b) The galaxy that the Sun is in is one of **billions** of galaxies in the Universe.
(c) Other stars in other galaxies are so far away from Earth that the distances are measured in **light years**.

4

Object	...	...	...	Explanation
Earth	...	...	...	Doesn't give out light. Fairly small diameter.
Galaxy	...	...	...	**Very large diameter.**
Planet	...	...	...	**Doesn't give out light. Fairly small diameter.**
Star	...	...	...	**Larger than Earth, but smaller than a galaxy. Gives out light.**

ages 107-108 — Dapper Day, Nifty Night ınd Super Season Questions

Quick Fire Questions

Q1 The tilt of the Earth's axis causes seasons.

Q2 365 ¼ days / 1 year.

Q3 The hemisphere in which it is winter is tilted away from the Sun, so it spends less time in sunlight than in darkness.

Q4 24 hours / 1 day.

Practice Questions

Q1 (a) E.g. the Earth is rotating on its axis. As it rotates, Astana is moving into the dark area and out of the light of the Sun.
(b) **B** — It is midday.
KL — The Sun has just set.

Q2 (a)(i) The time it takes the Earth to orbit once around the Sun.
(ii) It takes 365¼ days for the Earth to orbit the Sun. We say a year is 365 days, so a year with an 'extra' day is needed every fourth year.
(b)(i) B
(ii) A
(c) The daylight lasts for less time.
The daylight is spread over a larger area.
(d) At the same time that the northern hemisphere is tilted away from the Sun, the southern hemisphere is tilted towards it.

Q3 If the Earth was not tilted, the amount of sunlight each hemisphere receives would not vary as the Earth orbits the Sun. So the amount of sunlight falling on any given point on the Earth's surface would be the same throughout the year.

SHQA32 £2.00 (Retail Price)

www.cgpbooks.co.uk